celtic daily
readings

Also available from HarperCollins*Publishers*

Celtic Daily Prayer

CELTIC DAILY READINGS

READINGS

THE COLMAN SERIES

From the Northumbria Community

■ HarperCollins*Publishers*

HarperCollins*Religious*
part of HarperCollins*Publishers*
77-85 Fulham Palace Road, London W6 8JB
www.christian-publishing.com

First published in Great Britain in 2001 by
HarperCollins*Religious*

10 9 8 7 6 5 4 3 2 1

A catalogue record for this book
is available from the British Library.

ISBN 0 551 03267 7

Printed and bound in Great Britain by
Omnia Books Ltd, Glasgow

CONTENTS

Invocation of the Holy Spirit   vii

INTRODUCTION   ix
Daily Office   x
Colman   x
The readings   xii
Using the readings on a daily basis   xv
Celtic?   xv
Calendar of Saints' days and festivals   xvi

THE COLMAN SERIES OF DAILY READINGS   1
January:
Retrospective   1
February:
Past understanding   26
Broken gold   28
What gives you the right?   30
Gleanings   39
Final frontier   43
March:
With zeal for God   48
April:
The Book of the Law   72
Dietrich Bonhoeffer   79
Celtic insight   84

Tapestry   88
A journey around the island of pilgrimage   92
May:
God alone suffices   96
June:
Antony of Egypt   109
July:
Little brother of Jesus   135
August:
Journey through the Psalms   167
September:
Sayings of the Desert Fathers   194
October:
Walking on water   211
November:
Protective clothing   227
At His feet   241
December:
Jesse tree   247

FURTHER INFORMATION   280
Sources and acknowledgements   280
The Northumbria Community   283
Contacting the Community   286

QUICK REFERENCE GUIDE   287

Invocation of the Holy Spirit

Most powerful Holy Spirit,
    come down
        upon us
and subdue us.

From heaven,
    where the ordinary
        is made glorious,
    and glory seems
but ordinary,

bathe us
    with the brilliance
    of Your light
like dew.

This book is also dedicated to Clare Grimley who, just as it was going to press, died after a sudden illness.

We are on pilgrimage until our King and Master brings our boat gently to rest in His harbour and leads us quietly up the path of His Father's mountain.

Ant and Clare Grimley
(see entry for April 30 on page 95)

Teach me to live with eternity in view.
Tune my spirit to the music of heaven.
From Brendan – in exploration of a vision
in Celtic Daily Prayer

INTRODUCTION

Celtic Daily Readings provides a complete year of readings for use in prayer by an individual or group. In the Northumbria Community we are learning daily to ask the questions: 'Who is it that you seek?' and 'How then shall we live?' We recognise that, for us in the Community and for the many who have found great value in our Daily Office, these questions will not go away – and each day's reading is a reminder of their importance.

It is intended that this volume should stand perfectly well on its own, with each reading providing passages from Scripture and a 'thought for the day' to pray over, chew on and return to in meditation through the day. However, the book may also be taken as a complement to *Celtic Daily Prayer* – a collection of liturgies, meditations, prayers and readings from the Northumbria Community and published by HarperCollins (ISBN: 0551 03266 9). This latter volume contains two whole years of daily readings – they are called the Aidan and Finan series (see below for an explanation of these titles and why this book is called 'The Colman Series'). This present volume should prove particularly beneficial to those who have become used to those earlier series of readings, and would like material that is fresh, but from similar and familiar sources, and using the same general framework.

If, having used this book, you wish to know more about the Northumbria Community, we invite you to get in touch with us using the contact details on page 286.

Daily Office

The most important element within *Celtic Daily Prayer* is the
Daily Office – forms of Morning, Midday and Evening Prayer
which have become the heartbeat of the Northumbria Community.
Wherever and whenever possible the Office is said (or sung) by
companions in the Community as they go about their normal day's
work and life – which might be anywhere, as the Community is a
'dispersed' one, spread all over Britain and in other countries. The
Office provides a rhythm to the day which many find very helpful
as they struggle to seek God continually in the middle of the pressures and busyness of their lives. Morning and Evening Prayer
include opportunities for a daily reading, with its relevant scriptures and commentary, and for personal prayer. This is where the
three series of daily readings (Aidan, Finan, and now Colman) fit
into the wider structure, complementing the liturgies (very familiar
from their daily use) and the meditation for each day of the month
(old faithfuls, visited once a month). They introduce something
fresh and new into each day; but the thinking behind each reading
is always informed by the ethos, life, work and Rule of the
Northumbria Community.

Colman

The names given to the three series of readings are those of the
early bishops of Lindisfarne. Aidan, the first of these bishops, was
an Irish monk from Iona in the early seventh century who
answered a call from King Oswald of Northumbria to come to his
kingdom to assist in the task of evangelising his people. It was
Aidan who chose as his base the island of Lindisfarne (or Holy
Island, as it is more commonly called). Cut off by the rising tide
twice a day, it provided the isolation and retreat that Aidan and his
monks yearned for – but when the tide was out, the monks could
easily come and go about their work amongst Oswald's people.

Aidan's best-known successor was Cuthbert, the saint so dearly-beloved by the people of the north of England down the centuries and whose final resting place is in Durham Cathedral. However, there were other bishops in between: the first was Finan, who oversaw great missionary expansion throughout most of England from the base on Holy Island; and the next in line of succession was Colman, after whom this current series of readings is named.

Colman was bishop of Lindisfarne from 661 to 664. It was at this time that the Synod of Whitby took place – an important event in the development of the Christian church in Britain because it dealt with the question of whether the Celtic church, so strong in Ireland, Scotland and northern England, and which had developed somewhat independently of the church in Rome, should accept the authority of Rome over such contentious issues of the time as the correct date to celebrate Easter (see page 86 and also page 23). Colman spoke for the 'Celtic' party at the Synod – and seems to have been genuinely surprised by its outcome, which was favourable to the 'Roman' party. As a consequence, Colman withdrew to Iona, with a large company of English and Irish monks. Some years later he travelled on with them to his original home in the west of Ireland and founded a monastery on Inis Bofin in 667, and eventually a separate one for the English monks in Mayo.

There is perhaps a particular appropriateness in having a whole book dedicated to Colman. He seems to stand as a prophetic figure, determined to remain faithful to the old well-trodden paths understood and valued by John, Polycarp, Columba and by so many in between; and determined to set up 'waymarks' for those who would follow in days to come. Others remained behind in Northumbria after the Synod of Whitby to undertake the task of weaving the spirit of Celtic Christianity – its depth and spontaneity – together with the structure and conformity which the decision in favour of Rome had made inevitable.

Colman could not stay, and so removed himself from the stricture of the structure – but not to opt for an easy life. The spiritual disciplines typically undertaken by the Irish monks were demanding enough, designed to train Christian warriors, a *militia Christi*. Sadly, even the seeming utopia of his newly-founded community on Inis Bofin, far from the accommodation and compromise he feared in Northumbria, was disrupted by inevitable factional tensions. The English monks worked hard to put down new roots, while the Irish ones were anxious to undertake pilgrimages, and visit familiar places and faces before pulling their weight back at their little island home. Two communities emerged, and 'Mayo of the Saxons' became a famous seat of learning.

But Inis Bofin and Colman remind us to value our Celtic Christian heritage without romanticising it. Idealism must be earthed, with foundation-laying in bleak and beautiful conditions and surroundings. The spirituality of John, Columba, Aidan, Finan and Colman expressed itself in the hard slog of building up places to pray, live and offer hospitality; and the often harder work of persevering in building strong and loving relationships between believers, whilst serving the others God sends.

Colman climbed back upstream where he knew the waters were full of life; and he did not lack companions on the journey.

The readings

The readings in this book were originally circulated within the Community on a monthly basis as filofax inserts to a binder containing the Daily Office and other liturgies now included in *Celtic Daily Prayer*. They were written to build up the Community's awareness and knowledge of the many issues affecting individual lives – and indeed what it means to be a 'community' such as ours, seeking to both come apart into the recognition of God's presence and yet still be fully involved, as He is, in ordinary daily life. Just as Colman sought to 'set up waymarks' for those that followed, so the Community, through these readings, sought to revisit the 'waymarks' set up by others before us; and, hopefully, establish new 'waymarks' to help others following this road in the future.

Most months comprise a single theme or subject. However, not all of the original readings have stood the test of time, and so you will find that some months' readings comprise parts of different subjects that would originally have made up a full month. Some of the readings are very short and pithy; others are long and descriptive. If you find that the style of some is not appropriate to your present needs, do not feel under any obligation to work through the entire book on the prescribed days! It may prove equally valuable as a resource to dip into.

Some of the readings focus on the life or writings of a particular person whose life is important to the Community. **Antony of Egypt** (June) tells us something about the man who, in effect, initiated the monastic movement in the third century and was one of the original 'Desert Fathers' – whose influence reaches right down to us today, and some of whose wise sayings are brought to us in September. **Zeal for God** (March) is about Columbanus, an Irish monk who took the torch of the Christian gospel across continental Europe in the early seventh century – dark, turbulent years of invasion and conflict which replaced the civilisation and relative stability of the earlier Roman empire. **Little Brother of Jesus** (July) tells the remarkable story of an aristocratic Frenchman, Charles de Foucauld, who a century ago gave up everything to live in absolute poverty in his deeper search for God. His writings have come to have a special significance to the Community. **Dietrich Bonhoeffer** (April) provides a brief introduction to a man of great faith and integrity, a German Christian who was executed on Hitler's orders just before the end of the Second World War, and whose writings are an inspiration to all seeking to know 'How then shall we live?'. In October **Walking on water** draws from the writings of Madeleine L'Engle, a contemporary American Christian whose spiritual insights deserve wide attention.

Other readings focus on broader themes. **God alone suffices** in May brings us the insights of the 16th-century Spanish mystics such as Teresa of Avila (whose 'Bookmark' is used every day in the Community's Midday Prayer) and St John of the Cross. **Protective clothing** (in November) is about 'putting on Christ'. **Journey through the Psalms** takes us in August on a pilgrimage through the one section of the Bible we draw from in every single day's scripture readings – the songs of God's people everywhere. **The Book of the Law** in April provides us with some insights that reflect on the books of the Law that Moses brought to the Israelites in the desert. In February **Final frontier** makes us look at the subject of death and dying.

The **Retrospective** readings in January will be familiar to those who have used the Community's daily readings for a number of years: each day of the month a day's reading is taken from one of 31 months of previously-used readings. They provide a thread of continuity from previous publications into this present volume – and may well be a spur to revisit subjects that were important at the time but have been pushed into the background.

December's readings, **Jesse tree**, are somewhat different to the others – as evidenced by the fact that they are accompanied by line drawings. Some of the figures and readings remind us of Jesus through his forebears; some are rich in prophetic significance; and others tell the continuing story, reminding us of the covenant that Jesus the promised Messiah invites us all to enter into with Him. An old song says,

> Tell me the story often,
> for I forget so soon…

and

> I love to tell the story,
> for those who know it best
> seem hungering and thirsting
> to hear it, like the rest.

Today, when 'some have never heard', we find it is even more necessary to familiarise children and adults with the characters, stories and prophecies that take us through the human ancestry of Jesus and anticipate His nativity.

Using the readings on a daily basis

Each daily reading provides three scriptures: one from the Psalms; one from the Old Testament; and one from the New. If these readings are being used by a group as part of the Daily Office, it is good for different people to each read one aloud. A Bible may be left open until the next day at the scripture which seems most relevant to the needs of the moment, placed where it can easily be referred to.

Celtic?

Things Celtic are currently very much in fashion – but that was not so much the case when many of these readings were prepared. In order to make sense of the Community's journey, we needed to 'explore the old paths' to find what they could teach us. Often these are neglected in the headlong embrace of everything that is new. The 'old paths' all around us here in Northumbria resound with the startling testimony of the remarkable men and women who simply loved God and followed Jesus wherever the Spirit impelled and empowered them to go; they lit a fire in the so-called dark ages that brought warmth, culture, learning and, most of all, faith to vast numbers of people.

As we researched and studied these saints (and the Desert Fathers, who were their spiritual predecessors) we found many of the crucial lessons they taught gave us hope and coherence on our own journey: that people matter more than things, and relation-ships more than reputation; that prayer and action, contemplation and involvement, all belong together. Whilst resisting the temptation to hark back to some mythical 'golden age' (which probably never existed), we have attempted to be true to what we have learned and lived in the shadow of the Northumbrian saints and their teachers.

Not too much weight should therefore be given to the use of the word 'Celtic' in this book's title. The era of the Celtic saints is one of the key sources of the 'waymarks' that help the Community find its way as it journeys onwards – but the journey and the Community are about much more than that, as will be seen from these readings.

Calendar of saints' days and festivals

The names alongside the dates of many of the readings in this book refer to the saint or festival to be remembered on that day. A yearly calendar incorporating all these dates can be found in *Celtic Daily Prayer*, together with a summary of the lives of all the saints we remember through the year. To assist in finding helpful references within this book to individual saints and festivals, a quick reference guide has been provided on page 287; more extensive resources can be found in *Celtic Daily Prayer*.

January

RETROSPECTIVE

This month takes one reading from each of 31 previously used monthly series. For those who have walked the journey already, it will provide an opportunity to look back and see where they have been. For new travellers, it will provide information about the terrain traversed by those already on this road – and will hopefully give some coherence to what lies ahead.

January 1 *New Year Telemachus*

PSALM 29:2   I CHRONICLES 16:27–29   MATTHEW 2:1–3, 7–11

AT HIS FEET
O worship the Lord in the beauty of holiness!
Bow down before Him, His glory proclaim;
with gold of obedience and incense of lowliness,
kneel and adore Him, the Lord is His Name.

Low at His feet lay thy burden of carefulness,
high on His heart He will bear it for thee,
comfort thy sorrow, and answer thy prayerfulness,
guiding thy steps as may best for thee be.

Fear not to enter His courts in the slenderness
of the poor wealth thou wouldst reckon as thine;
truth in its beauty and love in its tenderness:
these are the offerings to lay at His shrine.

These, though we bring them in trembling and fearfulness,
He will accept for the name that is dear;
mornings of joy give for evenings of tearfulness,
trust for our trembling, and hope for our fear.

J. S. B. Monsell

January 2

PSALM 2:10–12   DANIEL 1:3–9   MATTHEW 17:24–27

TO A YOUNG DISCIPLE

> Be simple in faith but well trained in manners.

Augustine arrived in Canterbury in 597. When he first came to Kent he summoned bishops and teachers from the Celtic Church in Wales to a conference, at which they would discuss working together in the process of evangelizing the English. He remonstrated with them to change their traditions for Roman ones, but also prayed over a blind man who was duly healed.

To the second such conference the Welsh sent seven British bishops and many learned men, mostly from Bangor. (Bangor was a very important centre for faith and learning, reported to number 3,000 men, all schooled after the example of their abbot Comgall.) Before that second meeting, the Welsh Britons consulted a hermit for direction. He said of Augustine, 'If he is a man of God, follow him.' They asked him how they could tell. The hermit reminded them that Jesus said He was meek and lowly of heart. If Augustine were the same, it would be obvious that he bore the yoke of Christ and was offering it to them; but if he were harsh and proud, this was not God's doing and they should disregard him. The test should be this: that the British party arrive later than Augustine and his party, and observe whether he stood to greet them or insolently remained seated.

Not only did Augustine remain sitting down, but he began to lay conditions on their fellowship – that they should change the manner of their calculation of the date of Easter, their monastic tonsure, and their way of baptizing. Under such circumstances, they recognized that Augustine already despised what they stood for and would do so even more if they gave in to his demands. For want of manners, much healthy co-operation in the gospel was thus forfeited.

January 3

PSALM 50:2   HOSEA 10:12B   2 CORINTHIANS 4:6–7

WITHOUT WALLS
We are called to intentional, deliberate vulnerability.
The Rule of the Northumbria Community

I had a vision of a house. Every time a crack appeared in the wall, or there was damage in the house, I dashed out to repair it as quickly as I possibly could, like most of us do, so that the inside of the house was protected and kept safe from the weather and the storms. And the Lord said to me:

> This is what your Christian life is like. Whenever any cracks appear in the wall that's been built up around about you over the years by the world and by yourself you dash out and you fill in the cracks so that no one is able to see what is inside. But I want the world to be able to see what's inside. I want to be able to come in through the cracks into your life and I'm not going to fill them up either, I'm going to flow in and out of these cracks. So when you see the cracks appear in your life, don't rush out and fill them in. Let Me come in.

David Matches (introducing the song 'Let Me Come In' on his album Halleluya, I Feel Like Singin'*)*

January 4 *Juniper*

PSALM 42:8   DANIEL 6:10–11   PHILIPPIANS 4:8

BE THOU MY VISION
Thou my best thought
in the day and the night.

All kinds of things fill our thoughts, but when we think of Him, sanity enters the picture. It is as if the conductor takes his place at the rostrum: all the discordant sound, the tuning up and fidgeting, turns to silence; and then a melody, a full-bodied score in many parts, comes to birth in the very place where there had been chaos and confusion.

> Lord, I think many things. I have many thoughts.
> Let me not forget You, nor lose sight of You,
> even for a moment.

Thou, my best thought.

January 5

PSALM 55:22   GENESIS 26:34–27:10   JOHN 11:21, 40–44

JOURNALLING

It is strange how we can forget very important parts of our lives until we sit before a blank piece of paper and put them down one by one. In order to gain objectivity before any important decision, or many minor ones, it is valuable to take time to reflect.

Most of us bear heavy burdens much of the time. Those who open themselves to listen in depth to others hear a great deal of inner turmoil and confusion. For many people survival is victory, and a journal is a helpful tool for survival.

Giving expression in the written word to the feelings which appear about to overwhelm and possess us often gives us distance from them.

Morton T. Kelsey, Adventure Inward

January 6 Epiphany

PSALM 18:20–24, 30   I SAMUEL 18:28; 19:10   MATTHEW 5:38–44

THREE KINGS

David had a question: What do you do when someone throws a spear at you?

Does it not seem odd to you that David did not know the answer to the question? After all, everyone else in the world knows what to do when a spear is thrown at them. Why, you pick up the spear and throw it right back!

'When someone throws a spear at you, David, just wrench it out of the wall and throw it back. Absolutely everyone else does, you can be sure.'

And, in doing this small feat of returning thrown spears, you will prove many things: you are courageous; you stand for the right; you boldly stand against the wrong; you are tough and can't be pushed around; you will not stand for injustice or unfair treatment; you are a defender of faith, keeper of the flame, detector of all heresy; you will not be wronged. All of these attributes then combine to prove that you are also, obviously, a candidate for kingship. Yes, perhaps *you* are the Lord's anointed – after the order of King Saul.

There is also a possibility that in some twenty years after your coronation, *you* will be the most incredibly skilled spear-thrower in all the realm. And, most assuredly, by then...

...quite mad.

Gene Edwards

January 7

PSALM 139:18B   SONG OF SONGS 4:9   EPHESIANS 5:31–32

DEEPER LIFE

The pilgrim worried that sometimes he would not have much time to care for his love-relationship with God. Then the Lord spoke to him, and answered his unspoken question: 'Do you have only one minute? Hem it with quietness. Do not spend it in thinking how little time you have. I can give you much in one minute.'

The pilgrim sat by the water, and his dear Lord said to him: 'As the ripples of the river glance up to the light, let your heart glance up to Me in little looks of love very often through the day.'

Amy Carmichael

The old couple sat with each other in peaceable silence, and no signal was needed for the kettle to go on, the tea to be poured, the fire tended to.

'What do you find to do all the time after all these years?' someone asked the old lady. 'Don't you ever tire of each other's company?'

'Oh no,' she replied. 'You see, it's like this: I looks at him, and he looks at me, and we're happy together.'

January 8

PSALM 17:15   JOB 19:23–26   JAMES 5:10–11

THE INWARD JOURNEY

We usually learn about *Him* only during periods of adversity. Few, if any, of us really seek after a deep, intimate relationship with the Lord except (1) just before, (2) during, and (3) right after those periods of calamity, disaster, catastrophe, suffering and pain! That's true of the very sinful, the very religious, and … well … the rest of us!

I challenge the idea that suffering is first of all a punishment for our sins. If that were true, then every believer on earth would be hiding under a rock somewhere.

Job lowered his voice: 'It appears we have a God who has supreme confidence in His own judgement. Nor can He be persuaded to show a great deal of interest in explaining Himself. He keeps His counsel to Himself, it appears; nor is He perturbed in the least that we're perturbed about His not being perturbed. But,' said he, raising his index finger in a gesture of discovery, 'I didn't need to learn anything else. I saw Him. Getting questions answered seems rather a paltry thing in comparison to having *seen* Him.'

Christian stood there for a long time. 'It's hard to realize that that was the man Satan went after with such a vengeance!'

'Shhh,' said the angel, Messenger, 'he knows nothing of that!'

Gene Edwards, The Inward Journey

January 9

PSALM 89:8–16   LAMENTATIONS 3:40–41   GALATIANS 5:18–35

ENTER IN
Deserts, silence, solitude.

For a soul that realizes the tremendous need of all three, opportunities present themselves in the midst of the congested trappings of all the world's immense cities. But how, really, can one achieve such solitude?

By standing still!

Stand still, and allow the strange, deadly restlessness of our tragic age to fall away like the worn-out, dusty cloak that it is – a cloak that was once considered beautiful. The restlessness was considered the magic carpet to tomorrow, but now in reality we see it for what it is: a running away from oneself, a turning from that journey inward that all must undertake to meet God dwelling within the depths of their souls.

Stand still, and look deep into the motivations of life.

Stand still, and lifting your hearts and hands to God pray that the mighty wind of His holy Spirit may clear all the cobwebs of fears, selfishness, greed, narrow-heartedness away from the soul: that His tongues of flame may descend to give courage to begin again.

Catherine de Hueck Doherty, Poustinia

January 10

PSALM 52   AMOS 5:21–24   MATTHEW 7:21–23

DESERT FATHERS

Abba Agatho used to say:

> If you are able to revive the dead, but are not willing to be reconciled to your neighbour – it is better to leave the dead in the grave.

There was a certain Elder who, if anyone maligned him, would go in person to offer that person presents, if they lived nearby. If they lived at a distance, he would send presents by the hand of another.

January 11

PSALM 35:19–24   GENESIS 4:10–16   REVELATION 4:1

DEVOTED TO HIM

If the Catholicism that I was raised in had a fault, and it did, it was precisely that it did not allow for mistakes. It demanded that you get it right the first time. There was supposed to be no need for a second chance. If you made a mistake, you lived with it and, like the rich young man, were doomed to be sad, at least for the rest of your life. A serious mistake was a permanent stigmatization, a mark that you wore like Cain. I have seen that mark on all kinds of people: divorcees, ex-priests, ex-religious, people who have had abortions, married people who have had affairs, people who have had children outside of marriage, parents who have made serious mistakes with their children, and countless others who have made serious mistakes. There is too little around to help them. We need a theology of brokenness. We need a theology which teaches us that even though we cannot unscramble an egg God's grace lets us live happily and with renewed innocence far beyond any egg we may have scrambled. *We need a theology that teaches us that God does not just give us one chance, but that every time we close a door He opens another one for us.*

Ronald Rolheiser, Forgotten among the Lilies

January 12

PSALM 68:14–20   DEUTERONOMY 3:1–4   2 TIMOTHY 1:12B

HARD TO TELL

James Hudson Taylor, the great missionary to China, gave many testimonies to the enduring mercies of God in his work.

One instance of the care and faithfulness of God he could not but share with those at home. 'On Saturday morning,' he wrote, 'we paid all expenses and provided for the morrow after which we had not a single dollar left. How the Lord would care for us on Monday, we knew not, but over our mantelpiece hung two scrolls in Chinese characters: *Ebenezer* ('Hitherto hath the Lord helped us') and *Jehovah Jireh* ('The Lord will provide') – and He kept us from doubting for a moment. That very day the mail came in a week before it was due, and Mr Jones received a remittance for 214 dollars. So once again we thanked God and took courage.'

The defeat of Og, King of Bashan, was very significant to the people of God. The God who gave them victory over Og would help them against any other enemy too. The one word 'Og' summed up for them the message of both Hudson Taylor's banners!

January 13 Hilary of Poitiers Kentigern

PSALM 104:23   ISAIAH 43:21   COLOSSIANS 3:17

ASK FOR THE OLD PATHS
The first two years of Columba's residence in Iona were spent in learning the language, tilling the soil, training followers, and generally organizing the community. The days were filled with prayer, study and manual labour, and in this last Columba, with his great spiritual and intellectual gifts, was always ready to share. In dairy, granary, or in the fields, each worshipped God in his appointed tasks, and made his toil a sacramental thing ... The secret of the early Celts lay in this, that they linked sacrament with service, altar with hearth, worship with work.

F. M. McNeill/Troup

For us, too, it is important to discover the rhythm of praying as we work and praying through our work. Sometimes a simple manual task can even assist the praying heart in its focus.

Prayer-baskets were woven simply out of reeds as monastics framed their prayers. The simplest task can become a prayer-basket for us.

January 14

PSALM 17:1   SONG OF SONGS 1:5   MATTHEW 11:29–12:1

ALL YOUR CREATURES
The Prayer of the Cricket

O God,
I am little and very black,
but I thank You
for having shed
Your warm sun
and the quivering of Your golden corn
on my humble life.
Then take – but be forbearing, Lord –
this little impulse of my love:
this note of music
You have set thrilling in my heart.
Amen.

Carmen Bernos de Gasztold, Prayers from the Ark

January 15 *Ita Paul of Thebes*

PSALM 108:1   ISAIAH 30:9–11   JOHN 16:33

CALEB THE OVERCOMER
We are always prone to think that our lot is the hardest; that no one suffers quite as much as we; that there is some excuse for us because of circumstances so much more difficult than those of others. We are quite persuaded that no one could be victorious under the same circumstances.

Let us consider the circumstances under which Caleb lived those forty years in the wilderness. First let us see what it meant to him physically. Think of the exhausting weariness of body caused by those marches and counter-marches.

There were days, months, years of futile, aimless wandering, always going and never getting anywhere. There was the still more wearying work of war. Over against this Caleb had continually in his imagination the promised land of Canaan.

Then there were the physical deprivations he was compelled to endure. To his completely surrendered soul the daily manna was ever sweet and palatable we may be sure. But it couldn't compare with the milk, honey and fruit – the abounding plenty of the promised land.

Then to such a home-lover as Caleb, what must the forty years of homelessness have meant to him? And with Hebron, his rightful home, ever in his memory and vision!

In spiritual imagination Caleb had written the words MY OWN upon the gateposts of Hebron when he went to search out the land. Yet for forty years he was deprived of the peace and plenty, the sweetness and the satisfaction of Hebron.

But perhaps hardest of all to bear was the useless waste of life as it might legitimately have seemed to a wholly yielded person. Think of those rare years of middle life that might have been spent in the cultivation and use of his rightful inheritance, sacrificed to what seemed to be mere existence.

Ruth Paxson

January 16

PSALM 131:2   JUDGES 16:29–30   ACTS 7:55–60

CONTAGIOUS COMMUNITY

Suddenly Stephen was standing in the middle of the room
gazing at the ceiling, his whole being transfixed, his face
glowing with the glory of God. First-century believers had
a disconcerting way of stepping outside of the confines
of time and space. This was one of those holy moments.
Spellbound, Stephen stands innocently marvelling, oblivi-
ous to everyone else in the room. Suddenly he shouts out at
what he is seeing: 'Look ... I see heaven; it is opened! I see
the Son of Man standing at the right hand of God.'

That did it, the whole courtroom went wild. Madness
broke out. Men vaulted over benches and chairs. Everyone
in the room rushed towards Stephen, putting their hands
over their ears as they went, a sign that they could not bear
to hear another word of blasphemy from his mouth. It was
a scene of utter insanity. All judicial dignity, form, and position dissolved. There was nothing in the room but a crowd
gone wild, intent upon one thing: the death of Stephen.

Gene Edwards

And casting him outside the city, they stoned him. The
Lord, too, who chose us out of the world for His heavenly
kingdom and glory, suffered outside the gate, like Stephen,
who, as though he were a stranger to the world, was stoned
outside the city.

For he had no permanent city here, but with his whole
heart he sought the city to come. And falling on his knees
he cried out with a loud voice saying, 'Lord, do not hold
this sin against them.' For himself he prayed standing up,
for his enemies he knelt down. Because their iniquity was
so great it called out for the greater remedy of falling upon

his knees. His zeal was such that he openly reproached his captors for their fault in lacking faith, and he burned so with love that even at his death he prayed for his murderers.

Bede

As the witnesses raised the heavy stones above their heads and hurled them down into the pit, the first martyr of church history very simply slipped to his knees and fell quietly asleep.

Gene Edwards

January 17 Antony of Egypt

PSALM 31:24   JOSHUA 24:8–9   JOHN 6:67–68

A JOURNEY AROUND THE ISLAND OF PILGRIMAGE
Skellig Michael
We found ourselves alongside ten sea-strangers on an open boat cutting into the waves of the Atlantic off County Kerry. This day brought sharp summer weather and the untroubled Skelligs beckoned us outwards. Yet, with our necks strained looking up and up at these chunks of rock, the first wet of rain mixed with sea hit our tanned skin. We were here at Skellig Michael, but so too was the cold biting rain that drives out any romantic delusion of a sun-bathed monastery with well-fed monks. At least we, unlike those monks now long-flown this precarious nest, were well-protected with artificial skins.

We began the climb to the top, using the several hundred stone carved steps, more concerned with the wet cold and our safety, unthinkingly tramping on workmanship equivalent to the Gallarus Oratory.* Time soon became meaningless and the sea disappeared from view in the mist.

The home-like beehive cells of the monastery seemed strange in their stillness; but our own inner noise invaded their privacy. Huddled, like primitives, around a non-existent fire, we wondered what it might have been like to live here. But we were the ones who couldn't face the reality outside: the guide, like the monks before her, guarded this precious monastery unaware of the cold – something deeper kept them warm.

Ant and Clare Grimley

*The best-preserved Celtic building in the British Isles, on the Dingle peninsular.

January 18

PSALM 122:3–5   JEREMIAH 8:11   MATTHEW 6:33

SHALOM

Those who are called to be custodians of God's truth and guardians of the well-being of others carry a God-given responsibility. Like the sentry on the walls of medieval cities they are to be concerned for the safety and welfare of the community, and can only cry out 'all is well' when no danger threatens. But danger comes from within as well as from the outside, and the people of God have to probe deeply to ensure that the real foundations for shalom are in place. Just as war marks the absence of shalom between nations, injustice is the measure of the absence of shalom within society.

Kitty Hay

January 19

PSALM 117   DEUTERONOMY 6:5–6   REVELATION 3:14–19

COMPANIONS ON THE CHANGEFUL WAY

A single person truly on fire with the love of God is more useful than many souls if they are tepid.

Teresa of Avila

Fill Thou my life, O Lord my God,
in every part with praise:
that my whole being may proclaim
Thy being and Thy ways.

Horatius Bonar

January 20

PSALM 63:1–2, 7   PROVERBS 1:7   MARK 13:33–37

SMALL BEGINNINGS

The world gives itself
up to incessant activity
merely because
it knows of nothing
better.
The inspired man
works among
its whirring wheels
also; but he knows
whither the wheels
are going,
for he has found
the centre
where all is
stillness…

Paul Brunton

January 21

PSALM 109:22   JOB 1:21   ROMANS 8:22–26

JESUS OF THE SCARS

The inward journey involves pain, intolerable pain. According to John of the Cross, once we stop trying to run away from our loneliness, and stop trying to fill our thirsty caverns with counterfeit and pseudo-solutions, we enter for a time into a terrible raging pain, the pain of purgatory, the pain which is felt when we cut ourselves off from pseudo-supports and take the plunge inward, into the infinite mystery of ourselves, reality and God. Eventually this journey leads to a deep peace, but in the early stages it causes intolerable pain. Why?

Because we have stopped using anaesthetic. We have stopped numbing, drugging, distracting, and deflecting our lonely thirst. Thus, deprived of anaesthetic, and of the cellophane covering our superficiality, we can enter and feel fully our own depth. We face ourselves for the first time. Initially this is very painful. We begin to see ourselves as we truly are, infinite caverns, satiable only by the absolutely non-counterfeit, infinite love. We see too how, up to now, we have not drawn our strength and support from the infinite, but have drawn upon finite things. We realize that we must shift our life-support system – and the process of that shift is very painful.

Ronald Rolheiser, The Restless Heart

January 22

PSALM 119:129–132   HABAKKUK 2:14   JOHN 7:37–39

WITH UNDERSTANDING

Jesus stood up and said, 'Whoever is thirsty, let them come to Me and drink, and drink, and drink.'

O Lord, Your word enters and lets in the light. It gives understanding to the simple.

Open-mouthed and longing we come to You. To whom else shall we go? You have the words of eternal life. We have believed, some of us recklessly, some of us hesitantly, but we *have* believed, and have come to know that You are the only one who can satisfy our thirst.

> I am an emptiness for Thee to fill;
> my soul a cavern for Thy sea.

George Macdonald

January 23

PSALM 101:4–5   PROVERBS 30:12–13   JOHN 8:3–9

IONA

'Pray for me. I ask you, my brothers and sisters, to pray for me.' If ever you go to a black pentecostal church, that is a phrase you might hear almost every person use when they stand up or come forward to testify. Sometimes it is just like punctuation, not heartfelt at all, but even then it is still an important reminder.

If you attend Mass you will say, 'I ask ... all the angels and saints and you, my brothers and sisters, to pray for me to the Lord our God.'

George MacLeod, founder of the Iona Community, echoes the same words as he quotes the old spiritual:

It's not my brother or my sister
but it's me, O Lord:
standing in the need of prayer.
We are so warm in our own self-esteem
that we freeze the folks around us.
We get so high in our own estimation
that we stand isolated on a mountain-top
of self-righteousness.
That is why You came, Lord Jesus:
not to save the lecherous but to turn
the righteous to repentance.
And it is me, O Lord.

From Where Freedom Is and Laughter

January 24

PSALM 18:30–36   HABAKKUK 3:17–19   LUKE 19:37–41

CONSIDER MY MEDITATION

I'm not defeated. I'm an overcomer. I want to live to give glory to
You, God. All creation resounds with Your praise and longs to be
finally reconciled. I am part of Your purposes.

You cause my heart to soar like an eagle,
You teach my feet to conquer like a deer.
All I survey shall echo with Your praise, and Lord,
I know that *I* must know You here.

You place a reservoir within my heart, Lord,
that all my tears
would come from a different place:
that all my ways would minister Your grace
to those who long
to see Your face.

Teach us, Lord, to cry with Your tears, as well as our own.

January 25

PSALM 113:3   GENESIS 49:33   EPHESIANS 3:16–19

AIDAN

Aidan seemed even closer to heaven as his death approached –
the land, once a spiritual desert, has been irrigated by springs of
life coming from Lindisfarne.

> As the setting sun
> flings back its parting splendour,
> and illuminates the heaven
> it leaves with an unearthly light;
> not otherwise, when sinking to its rest,
> the sainted soul, its mundane labours past,
> reflects a splendour from the world
> unseen by mortal eyes –
> so glorious
> that it holds in wondering admiration all around.
>
> Such was the death of Aidan.
> His poor frame shrunk
> with much fasting and long travelling,
> no further would it bear him to and fro
> on works of mercy, and for others' good,
> and yet the more the outward man decayed
> the inward man grew stronger
> and it seemed to watching brethren that,
> though yet he lived on earth,
> his conversation was in heaven.

Arthur Wright, Life of St Aidan

January 26

PSALM 60:4   MICAH 5:2   LUKE 24:32

CROSSROADS

I read Isaiah 53 in the Old Testament and found it to be an absolutely uncanny description of Jesus being crucified – and yet it was written more than 700 years beforehand. In all, there are about five dozen major prophecies concerning the Messiah, and the more I studied them, the more difficulty I had trying to explain them away.

My first line of defence was that Jesus may have intentionally manoeuvred His life to fulfil the prophecies so that He would be mistaken for the long-awaited Messiah. For instance, Zechariah 9:9 foretold that the Messiah would ride a donkey into Jerusalem. Maybe when Jesus was getting ready to enter the town, He told His disciples, 'Go fetch Me a donkey. I want to fool those people into thinking I'm the Messiah because I'm really anxious to be tortured to death!'

But that argument fell apart when I read prophecies about events that Jesus never could have arranged, such as the place of His birth – which the prophet Micah foretold 700 years in advance – and His ancestry, how He was born, how He was betrayed for a specific amount of money, how He was put to death, how His bones remained unbroken (unlike the two criminals who were crucified with Him), how the soldiers cast lots for His clothing, and on and on.

That was impressive enough, but then in the book I was examining Stonor analysed 48 prophecies. His conclusion was that there would be one chance in ten to the 157th power that would come true in any one person in history. That's a number with 157 zeros behind it!

I did some research and learned that atoms are so small that it takes a million of them lined up to equal the width of a human hair. I also interviewed scientists about their estimate of the number of atoms in the entire known universe. And while that's an incredibly large number, I concluded that the odds of 48 Old Testament prophecies coming true in any one individual are the same as a person randomly finding a single predetermined atom among all the atoms in a *trillion trillion trillion trillion billion* universes the size of our universe!

Jesus said He came to fulfil the prophecies. He said, 'Everything must be fulfilled that is written about Me in the Law of Moses, the Prophets and the Psalms.'

Lee Strobel, Inside the Mind of Unchurched Harry and Mary

January 27

PSALM 131:2   JEREMIAH 17:7-8   PHILIPPIANS 4:12-13

GIFT FROM THE SEA

We have so little faith in the ebb and flow of life, of love, of relationships. We leap at the flow of the tide and resist in terror its ebb. We are afraid it will never return. We insist on permanence, on duration, on continuity; when the only continuity possible, in life as in love, is in growth, in fluidity – in freedom, in the sense that dancers are free, barely touching as they pass, but partners in the same pattern. The only real security is not in owning or possessing, not in demanding or expecting, not in hoping even. Security in a relationship lies neither in looking back to what it was in nostalgia, nor forward to what it might be in dread or anticipation, but living in the present relationship and accepting it as it is now.

Anne Morrow Lindbergh, Gift from the Sea

January 28 Canaire

PSALM 36:7–9   PROVERBS 17:1   MATTHEW 7:25

THE HOUSE THAT JOHN BUILT

King Oswy needed the Whitby Synod to settle once and for all which way Easter should be calculated. A small enough matter, but emotive because of conflicting loyalties involved and declared.

Colman spoke with pride for the Celtic side, declaring their loyalty to John the apostle, who had ruled that Easter should continue to be calculated in accord with Jewish reckoning. It had always been so, and Columba and others before and since had not seen fit to question this. It would do well enough.

Wilfrid, instead of arguing for the expectancy of united practice of some kind, spoke rudely of Columba and deprecatingly of the entire Celtic tradition. His six years on Lindisfarne had apparently not taught him to respect his betters, nor had his time away taught him manners.

Instead he employed an ingeniously simplistic argument: Peter holds the keys to the kingdom of heaven, yes? And you suggest that the king today should make a decision that will honour John in precedence over Peter?

Oswy the king felt left with no choice. It was not wise for someone who had lived a life that was at best only intermittently holy to risk the displeasure of the door-keeper of heaven itself.

Thus Wilfrid in Northumbria brought devastation on much that had been built by Oswald and Aidan in the name of John and Columba. What would remain, or be built again in the same spirit of the gospel?

January 29

PSALM 84:10–12   2 KINGS 23:4   LUKE 14:10A

DOOR-KEEPERS

As for me, I shall take my old accustomed place,
near enough to God to hear Him, and know He is there,
but not so far from others as not to hear them,
and remember they are there, too.

Where? Outside the door –
thousands of them, millions of them.
But – more important for me –
one of them, two of them, ten of them,
whose hands I am intended to put on the latch.
So I shall stand by the door and wait
for those who seek it.
'I had rather be a door-keeper...'
So I stand by the door.

Samuel Moor Shoemaker

January 30

PSALM 45:1   LEVITICUS 26:2–3   ROMANS 8:26

CHOSEN PEOPLE

There is a story told about a Jewish farmer who, through
carelessness, did not get home before sunset one Sabbath
and was forced to spend the day in the field, waiting for
sunset the next day before being able to return home.

Upon his return home he was met by a rather perturbed
rabbi who chided him for his carelessness. Finally the rabbi
asked him: 'What did you do out there all day in the field?
Did you at least pray?'

The farmer answered: 'Rabbi, I am not a clever man. I don't know how to pray properly. What I did was simply to recite the alphabet all day and let God form the words for Himself.'

When we come to celebrate we bring the alphabet of our lives. If our hearts and minds are full of warmth, love, enthusiasm, song and dance, then these are the letters we bring. If they are full of tiredness, despair, blandness, pain and boredom, then those are our letters. Bring them. Spend them. Celebrate them. It is God's task to make the words!

Ronald Rolheiser, Forgotten among the Lilies

January 31

PSALM 36:5   JEREMIAH 33:3   REVELATION 3:8

STANDING IN THE SECRET

A number of years ago, my friend Nigel painted a beautiful picture of a boy shooting lots of paper aeroplanes into the sky. They are all being directed at the same place high in front of him, and each falls to the ground again. The ground is covered with snow, and the sky with thick cloud, but in one place only a clearing has appeared and the deep blue of the night sky can be seen through it. It has become the gateway to heaven.

So often our prayers, and other initiatives taken in blind obedience to the Spirit, seem as pointless as shooting paper aeroplanes into the sky – but the eyes of faith know that it is no coincidence that that will be the place where the clouds clear and heaven penetrates earth's concerns.

Andy Raine

February

PAST UNDERSTANDING

February 1 *Brigid's Day*

PSALM 122:6–8   ISAIAH 66:12A   PHILIPPIANS 4:5–7

Peace passes the understanding – it is not dependent on mental ability or agility. Peace is flowing – because God is flowing, even as the sun always shines. Our *perception* of the sun is that it stops shining at night. Peace is always flowing and is looking for a channel to flow through.

God is looking in our lives for the maximum outflow of His peace.

Rob Fawcett

February 2

PSALM 126:4   ISAIAH 43:18–19   LUKE 11:34

Healing of memories is important, because painful memories can come and wound us – they bleed us, preventing us temporarily from exuding the power of God. How can you cope with the pressures of today when you're taking an exhausting walk down memory lane? If we've given ourselves in love and been hurt, God wants to make that new in us again.

Rob Fawcett

February 3

PSALM 72:3   JOB 37:5–6   I JOHN 4:18

A slalom skier moves fast. We are skiers in the Spirit – not *slalom* but *shalom* skiers. Always moving on, whether we like it or not. There are two ways of doing it: to come screaming and kicking into where God wants us; or to come quietly, willingly.

The shalom skier bobs and weaves through the attacks of the enemy. The concentration required demands a base of the confidence which inner peace gives. We need to be adept – our peace is derived from having competence in our job, avoiding the obstacles. We need to know that we're in the right place at the right time.

Rob Fawcett

BROKEN GOLD

February 4

PSALM 29:2   PROVERBS 3:25–26   MATTHEW 2:7–11

> Thanks be to Thee, Jesu Christ,
> for the many gifts Thou hast bestowed on me,
> each day and night, each sea and land,
> each weather fair, each calm, each wild.
>
> I am giving Thee worship with my whole life,
> I am giving Thee assent with my whole power,
> I am giving Thee praise with my whole tongue,
> I am giving Thee honour with my whole utterance.
>
> I am giving Thee reverence with my whole understanding,
> I am giving Thee offering with my whole thought,
> I am giving Thee praise with my whole fervour,
> I am giving Thee humility in the blood of the Lamb.
>
> *Mary Gillies of Morar, Western Highlands*

February 5

PSALM 136:11–12   EXODUS 14:19–20   MATTHEW 2:12

> I am giving Thee love with my whole devotion,
> I am giving Thee kneeling with my whole desire,
> I am giving Thee love with my whole heart,
> I am giving Thee affection with my whole sense,
> I am giving Thee my existence with my whole mind,
> I am giving Thee my soul, O my God of all gods.
>
> I am beseeching Thee
> to keep me from ill,

to keep me from hurt,
to keep me from harm,
to keep me from mischance,
to keep me from grief,
to keep me this night
   in the nearness of Thy love.

Mary Gillies of Morar, Western Highlands

WHAT GIVES YOU THE RIGHT?

February 6

PSALM 10   ESTHER 6:1–12   ACTS 19:11–17

As an allegory, the book of Esther may be taken to be a teaching about Christ the King and His bride, and the evil plots of Haman the enemy. As a history, it clearly shows Haman's unreasonable jealousy of Mordecai as the initial inroad for Satan, who used him to plan the extermination of the Jews.

In this part of the story Haman seeks honour for himself – and sees those very honours conferred upon Mordecai instead.

It is like the verse in Genesis 50:20 where whatever evil is intended against God's chosen is able to be turned to good.

Every curse becomes a blessing to the people of God's choosing. And so in Numbers 23 Balaam the prophet says, 'God is not a man that He should lie, or go back on His word. He has told me to bless and now He has made good the blessing – I cannot revoke it.' Daniel 11:32 promises that the people who know their God shall be strong and stand firm.

Jesus promises in John 12:26: 'Whoever serves Me, the Father will honour.'

February 7

PSALM 68:1–6   ESTHER 7:1–10   LUKE 11:24–26

Esther has prepared herself to come into the king's presence and ask for his mercy – not just for herself, but for the people she represents. She intercedes on their behalf. The enemy is put to shame and falls foul of his own machinations – captivity is taken captive!

It is important that we do not underestimate Satan's persistence, and his jealousy of any whom God honours. For instance, research has shown that Adolf Hitler and his closest associates were occultists, and their systematic plan to exterminate the Jews is referred to in their internal memoranda as Operation Haman. Hitler wrote that they must resume the task that Haman had been raised up to fulfil, but which had been interrupted before its completion.

February 8 Elfleda

PSALM 149:4–9   DANIEL 10:10–19   MATTHEW 18:18

Satan will sometimes do all that he is allowed to thwart the purposes of God – but we underestimate the contribution that our prayers can make in defeating the devices and schemes of the enemy. Territorial spirits do have influence on, or by default have jurisdiction over, areas and their inhabitants – but the faithful prayer of even one person can swing the balance in spiritual conflict.

God heard and answered Daniel's prayer immediately, but the enemy intercepted and delayed the answer. Daniel's persistence in prayer won the day, however: 'I am not defeated and I will not be; God sends *His* angels and they fight for me.'

An ancient prayer says:

> St Michael the archangel,
> defend us in battle;
> be our safeguard against
> the wickedness and snares of the devil.
> May God rebuke him, we humbly pray,
> and do thou, O prince of the heavenly host,
> by the power of God, cast into hell
> Satan and the other evil spirits
> who prowl through the world
> seeking the ruin of souls.

February 9 Teilo

PSALM 123:1–2   EXODUS 21:2–6   LUKE 17:7–10

Why do we call God 'Lord' if we don't make it our business to please Him first of all? If Jesus isn't Lord of all, then really He's not Lord at all in our lives.

A slave may be a slave by force of capture, or by financial circumstance, and in either case will still obey his lord and master's commands. Obedience is an action, but submission is an attitude.

The *doulos*, or 'love-slave', is one who could have been set free but chooses to stay with his master for ever – never again to be his own person, but to be marked as his master's instead. Such 'slaves' love their master more than the chance of independence.

Today, people's lives are all about being served by others, and a life given to pleasing someone else (God) runs completely contrary to the values of society, and even of much of the Church.

How often do our actions really have the motive of pleasing Him and knowing the smile of His approval? Or is all that we do really a thinly disguised way of merely pleasing ourselves?

> Christ has many services to be done;
> some are easy, others are difficult;
> some bring honour, others bring reproach;
> some are suitable to our natural inclinations and temporal
>   interests;
> others are contrary to both.
> In some we may please Christ and please ourselves,
> in others we cannot please Christ except by denying
>   ourselves.

From the Methodist Covenant Service

February 10

PSALM 146:5–7   GENESIS 27:1–36   LUKE 15:25–31

Jacob so valued his father's blessing that he persuaded his brother to give up his birthright as first-born son (Genesis 25:24–34) and then followed through by usurping the blessing intended for Esau. It seemed all or nothing, and he would risk everything to get it. Cheat, twisted one or not, *God* seemed to like his attitude.

In the familiar prodigal son story, the father turns to the elder son and says, effectively:

> You are always with me, and all that I have is yours. All you had to do was ask. Have you been with me this long, and still you don't know me?

And Jesus says to us:

> Extravagance to a wild and careless degree is the characteristic of My Father and Me. I was never precise, calculating and sensible when it came to giving life and love for you on that dark hill. That is why I have the reputation (in heaven anyway!) of being the most extravagant person ever to walk the dust paths of this planet ... You cannot hoard yourself up for a rainy day, son, and justify it in the light of My teaching. You must give yourself extravagantly, for security in the wisdom of your own economic prowess is directly opposite to the extravagance of My Father who revels in feeding birds, cultivating grass and inventing flowers simply because ... because ... because He enjoys doing it.
>
> *Philip Streeter,* You Are So Extravagant, Jesus

February 11 Caedmon

PSALM 37:1–11   LEVITICUS 18:24–29   ROMANS 8:18–25

Maybe it is too obvious to state that our sin even affects the land. No sin is ever strictly private, and the destiny of the whole created order is inextricably linked with our own.

The millennial prophecies talk about a time when the lion and lamb will lie down together. Disease seems to have been a consequence of the fall of humankind, and Satan (or one of his cohorts?) is dubbed Beelzebub, lord of the flies. The trees will clap their hands as God's words come to pass (Isaiah 55:11–13). Rainfall and cloud coincided with accumulated judgement, so that the rainbow Noah saw could well have been the first (Genesis 2:5–6). From that time, the length of days (i.e. people's age) was greatly diminished.

Jesus said that, if His disciples did not praise Him, the rocks and stones would cry out in their place (Luke 19:39–40). Even now the whole of creation waits on tiptoe to see if we will grow up and become 'sons', part of the family business at last! Saints and angels watch us endure conflict or run the race, and cheer us on (1 Corinthians 4:9 and Hebrews 12:1).

Our choices really do matter.

February 12

PSALM 19:7–14   AMOS 3:7–8   JOHN 15:9–15

> Your word have I hid in my heart that I may not sin against You.
>
> *Psalm 119:11*

The words of Jesus are words that bring life. We spend time in His presence, and often we hear nothing. Yet His presence has spoken to us, impressed us somewhere deep in our being. Often we may feel nothing, and we have only the discipline of choosing to spend time, putting ourselves in His presence. It is this action that makes it possible for Him to include us in His purposes. We slowly grow to know His ways, to recognize His hand at work in our circumstances and in the lives of others. We know when He is near. We love His appearing.

The silence is a desert – not always an oasis – and it is often dry as dust, but we can come out of that desert leaning on our Beloved (Song of Songs 8:5). What we have heard in a whisper we are ready to shout from the housetops.

We emerge from apparent deadness and silence and find that we have heard from God after all. The mercies of God are not for ourselves alone.

> In your hearts sanctify Christ as Lord. Always be ready to make your defence to anyone who demands from you an account of the hope that is in you.
>
> *1 Peter 3:15*

February 13

PSALM 133   I SAMUEL 18:1–4   LUKE 22:14–20

In Jewish tradition, various customs were familiar and understood by everybody. One of the most important was that of the *berith*, or covenant. This was not a light undertaking between two people. It gave them mutual access to property, and the enemy of one became the enemy of the other. A covenant mistakenly entered into could be your ruin. Saul realized this, and feared Jonathan forfeiting the throne through the *berith* he had made with David.

The ceremony was simple: an exchange of clothes or arms, a shared meal of bread and wine, and then the words of promise:

This is my body, I give it to you.
Whoever touches you touches me.
I will give my life for you if necessary.
This is my blood I am willing to shed for you.

Every Jewish boy recognized those words instantly, but Jesus must have confused His disciples by using them as He raised the Messiah's cup and the unleavened bread of Passover. Jewish covenant-brothers walked together through the shed blood of an animal; other blood-brothers cut their wrists, mingled the blood, and rubbed dirt in until scars made it clear they were in covenant with someone.

Jesus was the Passover lamb who was slain, and we walk together through His shed blood – but He will always be known by the scars.

February 14

PSALM 23   2 SAMUEL 12:1–24   MATTHEW 13:34–35

God showed Nathan the situation, but that alone did not give Nathan the right to interfere. He had to make David see it first, and then turn David's own words round on him. David was very susceptible to this approach and Joab used a similar device years later (as recorded in 2 Samuel 14) to encourage him to be reconciled with Absalom.

David's ability to pick up and go on after the death of his child should not surprise us: the long waiting was over. It is hope deferred that makes the heart sick. He had already reached a place where he could respond with '*fiat*' – 'let it be'.

The song 'From a Distance' asks us to view the world from a God's-eye view, with the kind of caring He demonstrated as He suffered on the cross. One of the ways in which we are able to experience an objective view, or a different subjectivity, is through stories. They help us understand, even if only by isolating one element of the truth at a time.

Each person has his or her story, and we can learn much by listening. Reality and parable both mediate truth.

February 15

PSALM 78:10–22   NUMBERS 20:7–13   REVELATION 5

The people had been too fearful to enter the land, and now a new generation has grown up to replace them. It is nearly 40 years later, and again the people moan and complain. God will again give them water from the rock.

In Exodus 17:5–7 we read of how the rock would be smitten once and for all, and 1 Corinthians 10:4 tells us that Jesus was that rock. Here, Moses is told only to speak to the rock and water will come. He disobeys and, presuming to be angry with the people, strikes the rock. In doing this he is disqualified from entering the promised land himself. Having come this far, he is allowed to see the land, but cannot be trusted to lead the people in.

Our disobedience can never stop God loving us, but He cannot approve of sin and sometimes our actions prevent Him from selecting us as His instruments. God forgives us, but sometimes has to change plans when we fail Him, and give certain tasks to other people. Only He in His wisdom can judge when this is necessary. He alone is worthy.

February 16

PSALM 78:49–52   EXODUS 12:3–13   REVELATION 22:14

The blood of the lamb over the doorpost prevented the angel of death from taking those within. The first and truly begotten Son had already been given, so for those who trusted in the blood of the lamb their own firstborn need not be given over to death.

Jehovah Jireh: God had provided Himself a sacrifice (Genesis 22:13–14). Sin means death, and in order for the people to go free, a sacrifice was required. But death works backwards. God reveals 'a deeper magic from the dawn of time'. Hidden deep in eternity is a secret, more powerful than any knowledge: the Lamb slain before the foundation of the world (1 Peter 1:19–20).

The cross was *not* inevitable. Humankind might have chosen not to sin, but a cross had to be in the heart of God – that willingness to go, to suffer, to redeem – or He could never wisely have created people and given us the earth.

> Blessed are they that have washed their robes in the blood of the Lamb, that they may have access to the tree of life, and enter in through the gates into the City.
>
> *Revelation 1:5–6*

GLEANINGS

February 17 Finan John Hyde

PSALM 91:4A ISAIAH 53:2, 5 ROMANS 5:8

The love that emanates from the cross of Jesus is not something to be admired, adored, but is to be seized and lived under.

Ronald Rolheiser, Forgotten among the Lilies

February 18 Colman

PSALM 106:15 ECCLESIASTES 4:4 PHILIPPIANS 1:21–23

We focus on something we are missing, and desperately crave – a marriage partner, a certain friendship, a certain achievement, a certain prestige, a certain physical appearance, a certain frame or place to live in – and we relativize and belittle our own lives to the point of finding them unhappy and meaningless.

We live in brackets, waiting; always waiting for this certain something to come along and fulfil our lives. When this happens, a deep restlessness sets in.

Ronald Rolheiser, Forgotten among the Lilies

February 19

PSALM 51:6 PROVERBS 28:13 LUKE 15:28–31

It is a mistake to restrict sin to specific and somewhat outstanding acts, as though the rest of our acts (and inactivity is an act) when not God-centred are neutral. Rather is sin to be seen as an orientation, a more or less continual series of choices against what one knows in one's deepest heart is right. It is an evasion of life, a refusal to stand in the truth of one's being. This is the offence to God, that His beloved creatures, to whom He longs to give Himself, refuse this gift. This gift of His love is enshrined in the acceptance of ourselves and in life as it really is ... 'My life is in my hands' – this is true of each of us. *I can treasure every drop of my life or I can squander it, letting it drip through my fingers as something of no account.*

> **Sister Ruth Burrows,** Before the Living God

Socrates commented that 'the unexamined life is not worth living'. I suspect that our age would counter with 'the unlived life is not worth examining'.

> *Ronald Rolheiser*

February 20

PSALM 73:3–9   PROVERBS 16:18–19   LUKE 1:46–47, 51–52

Pride makes us cut a sorry figure, because we always fit its garment to a shape that is not our own.

> *Hugh Redwood,* Pines and Pitprops

February 21

PSALM 86:2–4   GENESIS 6:8–13;   7:1 HEBREWS 11:7

In the old Negro play *The Green Pastures*, 'de Lawd' walks among humankind and Noah says to Him sincerely:

I'm jes' ol' preacher Noah, Lawd, an' I'm yo' servant.
I ain't very much, but I'se all I got.

February 22

PSALM 34:14B   PROVERBS 16:5–7   MATTHEW 5:23–24

Forgiving is a bold choice for a peaceful heart.

February 23   *Polycarp*

PSALM 116:12–14   SONG OF SONGS 7:10   REVELATION 21:2–4

In *Molchanie – The Silence of God*, Catherine de Hueck Doherty describes a vision she had of the Church:

> There she stood, above the treeline, shining in the rays of the noonday sun. She was beautiful and simple, with her doors wide open, and into her streamed the rich and poor alike … I realized that she was the Bride of Christ … I knew that she was His beloved and that He was all tenderness, all love, towards her … Not only was she His beloved, but she served the people whom He loved, the poor. The people whom He had fed with loaves and fishes she now fed with bread and wine. From my soul rose an immense cry of adoration.

February 24

PSALM 145:1–14   DEUTERONOMY 10:19–21
    I CORINTHIANS 12:31B–13:1

The Lord told Catherine de Hueck Doherty:

> It is your business and others' to go forth, confronting people face to face, for that is the only way of bringing them to Me. For when you are face to face with them, you love them, and once you love them, then I can speak through you.

February 25

PSALM 51:13   JEREMIAH 1:7   ROMANS 10:14–15

To love to preach is one thing; to love those to whom we preach is quite another. It was said of St Francis that he went everywhere preaching the gospel, and sometimes he used words.

> When we come to the end of our pilgrimage and reach heaven, God will ask, 'Where are the others?'
>
> *Charles Peguy*

FINAL FRONTIER

February 26

PSALM 79:5–6   DEUTERONOMY 30:19   MATTHEW 22:8–14

There is a long list of Christian thinkers and writers who have
been 'universalists' – that is, who have held the view that at the
end of the day a loving God would be unable to allow so many
souls to be consigned to hell, eternal death, or even extinction. It
is perhaps inevitable that we speculate whether God has some
trump card up His sleeve that would enable (in Mother Julian's
words) 'all things' to be well and 'all manner of things' to be well.
We have no authority to teach this, however. The Scripture seems
clear that our future hinges on our response to God in this life.
The only small print we can read this side of the grave is the foot-
note which says that, if we lead others to stray by what we teach,
it would be better that a millstone be hung round our neck! It is,
after all, more than idle speculation. It is a matter of life and
death.

> Close the doors,
> they're just not coming.
> We sent the invitations out
> a long, long, long, long time ago.
> We're still gonna have a wedding feast
> big enough to beat them all.
> The greatest people in the world
> just wouldn't come, so now
> we'll just have to invite the small.
>
> *Keith Green*

> And now the end is near,
> and so I face the final curtain.
> My friend, I'll say it clear,

I'll state my case, of which I'm certain.
I've lived a life that's full.
I've travelled each and every highway;
but more, much more than this,
I did it my way.

From the song popularized by Frank Sinatra

God, can You be merciful and send
me off to hell and lock me in forever?

No, Pilgrim, I will not send you there,
but if you choose to go there,
I could never lock you out.

From The Singer *by Calvin Miller*

Decision is the key to destiny.

February 27

PSALM 78:2–3, 16–19   JOB 4:8   MATTHEW 13:24–43

All the world is God's own field,
fruit unto His praise to yield;
wheat and tares together sown,
unto joy or sorrow grown;
first the blade and then the ear,
then the full corn shall appear;
Lord of harvest, grant that we
wholesome grain and pure may be!

To love my sins, a saint appear,
to grow with wheat and be a tare,
may serve me while on earth below,
where tares and wheat together grow.

But soon the reaping time will come,
and angels shout the harvest home.

For the Lord our God shall come,
and shall take His harvest home;
from His field shall in that day
all offences purge away,
give His angels charge at last
in the fire the tares to cast,
but the fruitful ears to store
in His garner evermore.

Even so, Lord, quickly come,
bring Thy final harvest home;
gather Thou Thy people in,
free from sorrow, free from sin;
there, for ever purified,
in Thy garner to abide;
come, with all Thine angels, come,
raise the glorious harvest home.

Henry Alford/Joseph Hinchcliffe

February 28

PSALM 72:6–15   ISAIAH 11:4–10   REVELATION 20:2–3

Throughout the Old and New Testaments there are many references to 'last things': the return of Christ; the end of the world; the rapture of His people caught up to be with Him; terrible tribulation and a 1,000-year reign on earth when Satan is bound up – the millennium. What each of these passages mean, and how the events described in them will happen, and especially in what order, is the subject of much diverse opinion and controversy between Bible teachers and those they school in their views.

In simple terms, there are five basic views (with many variations in each):

1 **Postmillennialism** says that things are getting better and God's kingdom is spreading through the world with the preaching of the gospel. Some day soon, the knowledge of the Lord will flood the earth and the millennium will have begun. Eventually Christ will bring it to an end by returning in person as Judge and King of Kings.

2 **Amillennialism** does not recognize any need for a specific 1,000-year period to take place in order to fulfil Scripture. We are in the millennium now, while God's kingdom is 'already', as well as 'yet to come'. These are times when Satan is active on the earth, but bound in the sense that he is powerless to prevent the spread of the gospel. Christ will come back at the climax of the conflict between good and evil.

3 **(Classic) Premillennialism** teaches that at the end of the great tribulation Christ will return and reign on earth for 1,000 years.

4 **Pretribulationism** is a more recent form of premillennialism in which Christians expect to avoid going through the tribulation because they will be conveniently raptured just as it is about to begin.

5 **Confused but happy**: many Christians prefer not to think about the issue, on the grounds that all it does is cause arguments. (Their views on the relevant scriptures are admittedly muddled and inconsistent.)

What we believe does affect very strongly the way we live. If we think we will be imminently airlifted from this planet, then we will probably care little for the rainforests or the population explosion. If we talk of restoration, then we embrace positions of influence and affluence as 'only the beginning of ruling and reigning as the children of God'. If we believe that 'we could be the generation to bring back the King', we may devote our energies to evangelizing unreached language groups. And if we long for His appearing, we will keep our lives in order as a reflex action: we look for His smile of approval day by day anyway, not as an insurance policy.

CHRIST HAS DIED. CHRIST IS RISEN. CHRIST WILL COME AGAIN.

February 29

PSALM 50:4–6   DANIEL 12:2   I THESSALONIANS 4:16–17

When the trumpet of the Lord shall sound,
and time shall be no more,
and the morning breaks, eternal, bright and fair,
when the saved of earth shall gather
over on the other shore,
and the roll is called up yonder, I'll be there.

On that bright and cloudless morning,
when the dead in Christ shall rise,
and the glory of His resurrection share,
when His chosen ones shall gather
to their home beyond the skies,
and the roll is called up yonder, I'll be there.

Let us labour for the Master
from the dawn till setting sun,
let us tell of all His wondrous love and care;
then, when all of life is over,
and our work on earth is done,
and the roll is called up yonder, I'll be there.

James M. Black

March

WITH ZEAL FOR GOD

This month's readings take us through the life of Columbanus (also known as Columban or Columba – but not to be confused with Columba of Iona, who lived a little earlier), the most tireless of Celtic missionaries to Europe. Columbanus' writings (in Latin) are the earliest by an Irish monk that have come down to us. We also know about him from *The Life of Columban*, written by a Bobbio monk named Jonas. Jonas never met Columbanus, having joined the community three years after Columbanus' death, but he lived and worked with those who had.

March 1 *David*

PSALM 131:1–2   I SAMUEL 22:1–2   EPHESIANS 2:19–22

The Celtic missionary genius had produced individuals of outstanding energy and had given the world magnificent apostolic personalities. Of these Columbanus was probably the greatest.

Georges Goyau

Celtic monks travelled as wandering pilgrims (*peregrinati*) seeking the will of God through a life of asceticism, breaking down the last possible barrier between themselves and God – love of their own country – and making a total gift of themselves to God by voluntary exile. When they encountered the heathen, their wholeheartedness made them superb missionaries. But we must not think of this as planned mission endeavour. It was far more haphazard, a by-product essentially of their determination to follow the will of God.

Kate Tristram

Columbanus began his studies at the new monastery of Cleenish, on an island in Lough Erne, County Fermanagh, Northern Ireland. The monastery was begun by Sinell, who had been trained at Clonard. When Columbanus definitely decided to become a monk, however, he went to Bangor, on Belfast Lough. We must not imagine Bangor, or indeed any of the great Irish monasteries of the sixth century (and Bangor was one of the greatest), as early versions of the great medieval monasteries of Europe. It was much closer in appearance to the primitive monastic settlements of the Nile Valley, a collection of round wooden huts built around a small church and surrounded by an embankment.

When the Latin word *monasterium* was borrowed into the Irish language, it initially took the form *muintir*, which was applied not to the monastic buildings but to the people who dwelt in them. In short, for the Irish the monastery was the *community*, not the buildings.

March 2 *Chad*

PSALM 128:1–4   2 SAMUEL 11:2–4   GALATIANS 5:13–14

'It's all very well if you're one of these holy men who understands exactly what God expects of you.' This is how we think all too easily! But Columbanus had problems with his vocation, and was troubled about celibacy. *The Life of Columban* tells us he was a good-looking lad who attracted plenty of girls without trying (the kind of girls with great bodies and no hesitation) without even trying. Columbanus found this a struggle. He was aware of his own weakness, and increasingly disturbed by his own thoughts. He was given good counsel by a hermit woman, however, and decided to continue on the road to religious life.

March 3

PSALM 84:6–8   GENESIS 12:1   LUKE 12:49–50

Before he became a great missionary, it took time for
Columbanus to be trained as a good Christian and a good monk.
The fire of the gospel was already lit within him, but he still
waited until he was ready to embark on his *peregrinatio*. When he
left Ireland in around 590, he was nearly 50 years old. He went
with 12 companions, as was usual for Celtic missionaries.

Again, we must be careful not to have any idealized notions
about the monks' travels. *The Life of Columban* does speak about
faith and total confidence, but also about hesitation and indeci-
sion, times of anxiety.

Beginning on Breton soil, they went on to cross all of Gaul
(roughly the area of modern France) from north-west to east, until
they were given land in the Vosges hills, in the Frankish kingdom
of Austrasia and Burgundy. They established their first monastery
at Annegray and after some time, when there were too many
monks, they opened a new monastery at Luxeuil and a third at
Fontaines.

March 4 Owini

PSALM 16:7–8   NUMBERS 20:7–11   ACTS 2:42–47

Columbanus built his religious life on solitude. Many times he
left his community for a 'desert' life of fasting and prayer. It was
an experience of the powerful goodness of God, and also a victory over fears. The fears he defeated were sometimes of external
things, such as wild animals, and sometimes of things inside himself. He just had to go somewhere – not even very far from the
monastery – and find a good place, a cave, a wood, near a small
river, and then stay there for as long as he could, until his monks
absolutely needed him to return.

During the times of pilgrimage in his life, however, Columbanus seems to be different – more of a preacher or a prophet. This was not a different side of him, exactly, but the same zeal of his religious life expressed in preaching. Whenever he was on the move by choice or force of circumstances, he would teach the gospel truth to anyone he met. Of course, what he was speaking about was the relationship with God he enjoyed and discovered in his life as a hermit, and the Christian way of life he recommended was what he also experienced in his community of monks. This deep coherence between what he said and what he lived was the main source of his success as a preacher and as a monastic founder.

Columbanus' own example and personal achievements aside, the 'usual way of life' he established for his monks was to stay in the monastery and to share a communal life.

March 5

PSALM 55:17   DANIEL 6:10B   I THESSALONIANS 5:16–18

Columbanus decided to give his monks a written rule. For him, the spirit of recollection had to be nurtured by silence and led to the use of repeated prayers.

At the third (Terce – 9 a.m.), sixth (Sext – midday) and ninth (None – 3 p.m.) hours of the day, the monks assembled in the church to recite three Psalms with versicles, and these remained unchanged throughout the year. So also did the 12 Psalms recited at nightfall (Vespers – 6 p.m.) and midnight (Midnocht), but the 3 a.m. office varied with the time of the year, reaching its maximum of 36 Psalms during the long winter nights from November 1 until February 1. Saturday and Sunday mornings demanded double time in the church in preparation for the Lord's Day and the day of rest, so that during the winter months the community chanted the whole Psalter within these two nights. In nothing were the monks so minutely directed as in this daily chanting of the Divine Office. A cough, a laugh, a late arrival all had their own penalties, with the cook and porter given more leeway than the rest to allow for an unexpected guest.

The three houses were under the direct control of Columbanus himself, and he seems to have made Luxeuil the mother house of the group. According to Jonas, the community at Fontaines numbered 60 monks, and as Luxeuil was undoubtedly the largest of the three, it may be assumed that the total in the three houses came to over 200 monks.

> May we love You alone,
> desire You alone,
> contemplate You alone by day and night
> and keep You always in our thoughts.
>
> *Columbanus*

March 6 *Baldred   Billifrith*

PSALM 18:19–27   EZEKIEL 18:21–28   JAMES 5:16

> The more light that is shed by scholars on the period known as the Middle Ages, the clearer it becomes that it was thanks to the initiative and labours of Columbanus that the rebirth of Christian virtue and civilization over a great part of Gaul, Germany and Italy took place.
>
> *Pope Pius XI*

It was by their imposition of penances after private confession of sins, in the tradition of the Celtic penitentials, that Columbanus and his monks changed the whole discipline of the early Church, when they applied the system also to the laity.

Columbanus' cure for sin was the practice of the opposing virtue:

The talkative is to be punished with silence,
the restless with the practice of gentleness,
the gluttonous with fasting,
the sleepy with watching.

March 7

PSALM 27:1–3   I KINGS 19:9–18   MARK 6:14–29

A few years after Columbanus' arrival, King Childebert of Austrasia and Burgundy died and his kingdom was divided into two for his two sons to rule. Burgundy went to the son called Theuderich. As the boys were both too young to rule in person, their grandmother Brunhilde acted as regent. Later on this led to war, and in 612 Theuderich was the victor. His brother was killed at Brunhilde's order.

In the midst of all these events, Columbanus' role was that of a prophet. He reacted initially against the wayward life of the young king Theuderich, who had installed a number of concubines in the royal household and soon had four illegitimate children.

One day, Columbanus went to see Queen Brunhilde, who led out the four royal bastards to meet him. Columbanus asked who the children were. 'They are the king's sons,' she answered. 'Confirm them with your blessing.' It may be that Brunhilde's ulterior motive was to secure, in the eyes of the courtiers, approval of the young men who would one day press their claim to succeed their father. Whatever the reason, Columbanus refused to be associated with the ruse. 'You must know,' he thundered, 'that these will never hold the royal sceptre, because they were begotten in sin.' Then he stormed out of the palace. Columbanus had just won the queen's hatred.

Columbanus wrote:

Most loving Saviour,
may affection for You pervade our hearts.
May attachment to You
take possession of us all.
May love of You fill all our senses.
May we know Your love so great
that the many waters of these heavens
and land and sea will fail to quench it.

Brunhilde pressed for an investigation into Columbanus' monasteries, and was supported by the bishops. These bishops were tired of Columbanus' independence, especially his persistent use of the different dating for Easter. Finally, Theuderich rode out with a company of his followers to confront Columbanus in Luxeuil. The king demanded to know why entry into the more secluded parts of the monastery was not allowed to all. Columbanus replied that outsiders were not allowed to enter the living quarters of the servants of God, but that appropriate hospitality was provided for all such guests. The king demanded free entry for all to the whole monastic complex – 'if you wish to retain the rights of our generosity and our full support...' Columbanus answered that any such violation of the cloister would mean the end of the monastery. If Theuderich were responsible for this, Columbanus prophesied, it would soon be followed by 'the destruction of his kingdom and the scattering of his race'.

March 8 *Senan*

PSALM 27:4–5   EZEKIEL 43:4–11   HEBREWS 7:24–27

It is You who light my lamp; the Lord, my God, lights up my darkness.

Psalm 18:28

Give my lamp such a share of Your light, my Jesus, I pray, that its brightness may reveal to me the Holy of Holies, where You the eternal Priest of all eternity enter the portals of Your great temple, so that I may always gaze at, behold and desire only You. May I love and contemplate You alone, and may my lamp ever burn and shine before You.

Columbanus

March 9

PSALM 27:6   I KINGS 21:17–29   LUKE 10:5–11

In all his simplicity and tenderness, Columbanus was jealously shielded by an aversion to any display of sentiment. Yet in rare, unguarded moments, he was found playing with a little girl at her father's villa, or sending to one of his monks the kiss which he had omitted to bestow in the haste of exile. The poor, the sick and the unfortunate were drawn to him by his sharing of their common lot. Even criminals, released from their fetters, felt impelled to kneel beside him as he prayed, and the rough soldiers asked his pardon when they came to take him from Luxeuil.

The king's dispute with Columbanus had finally come to a head and he sent his own chamberlain, Count Bertechar, with an armed expedition under Captain Ragamund, to enforce Columbanus' expulsion. The community was in the church chanting the Office when the party arrived in Luxeuil. Bertechar and his men tried to persuade Columbanus to obey the king's command voluntarily, as they would otherwise be forced to carry out what was for them a very unpleasant task. The Irishman was unbending to the end, however: 'I left my native land for the love of Christ; I shall not leave this place unless I am forced to.' Then, ordering the community to continue chanting the Office after his departure, he raised his hand in blessing and gave himself up.

Bertechar's orders were that the Irish and Breton monks were to accompany their master, but those born in Gaul were to remain in Burgundy. Therefore, with a small group of fellow Celts – Deicola, Lua and Eunoc, probably Aedh and certainly Gall – Columbanus placed himself under the control of Captain Ragamund and his men. It was the year 610, almost two decades since the foundation of Luxeuil.

March 10

PSALM 27:7   JONAH 1:15–16   ACTS 27:9–26

In Jonas' narrative, the progress of Columbanus and his companions across what is now central France was marked by a series of remarkable and often miraculous happenings. Yet it must have been a very exhausting march for men who were no longer young. Columbanus himself was nearing 70, and Nantes was nearly 400 miles away.

On their arrival there Columbanus wrote what he thought would be his last letter on French soil to his monks in Luxeuil. It was a letter full of tenderness and resignation. He pointed out that he was being compelled by force to return to Ireland – yet he could have escaped, for even the guards seemed to wish it.

As the merchant vessel on which he and his companions were intended to sail for Ireland was preparing for her departure, Columbanus made an unusual request to the local ecclesiastical and civil authorities: 'Let all my companions and the baggage be put on board. I will take a small boat from the Loire as far as the open sea.' Was he perhaps trying to emulate those Irish monks who sailed off in an open boat without oars, leaving it to their Divine Master to guide them whither He wished them to go?

At all events, aid did come from the heavens. While Columbanus was still waiting at the mouth of the river, a storm blew up which drove the merchant ship aground. For three days the captain failed to refloat his vessel and then, taking it as a sign that he was not to co-operate in the expulsion of the monks from Gaul, he put them and their belongings ashore again. Friend and foe alike were convinced that God wished Columbanus to stay.

March 11

PSALM 115:4–8   JUDGES 6:23–32
        ACTS 9:18–20, 22–25; 19:11–31

Columbanus and his followers returned eastwards and eventually arrived at the border between what is now Germany and Switzerland. The Alemannic tribesmen in the neighbourhood, the only German tribe which had resisted Christianity, still worshipped Woden and Columbanus made a few converts among them. Unfortunately, the impulsiveness of Gall, who set fire to their temples and threw their offerings into the lake, spoiled his master's efforts. Learning of a plot to murder Gall, Columbanus decided to depart quickly, and the whole community was on the move once more.

At the point where the Upper Rhine flows into Lake Constance (Bregenz, now in Austria), they disembarked and found a ruined chapel dedicated to St Aurelia which had been converted into a pagan temple. Its restoration to Christian worship was to be their first task. Gall first preached to the crowd and called on them to turn away from the worship of the bronze images which they had fixed to the walls of the former church. He then took down the images, broke them with stones and threw them into the lake. Some of the people departed in rage, but others remained to worship Christ.

Then Columbanus blessed the water and sprinkled it around the building, while the monks walked in procession around it chanting Psalms. Finally Columbanus proceeded to the altar which he anointed with oil, and celebrated Mass.

March 12 Paul Aurelian

PSALM 27:8   GENESIS 1:26   MARK 1:35

> Shepherd Your people with Your staff,
> the flock that belongs to You,
> which lives alone in a forest
> in the midst of a garden land.
>
> *Micah 7:14*

On a wooded, rocky hillside near the village of Sainte-Marie-en-Chanois (near Luxeuil-les-Bains in Haute-Saône) one can still find today an eleventh-century chapel dedicated to St Columbanus. It stands beside the cave which, tradition has it, served as Columbanus' cell, where he used to retire periodically to be alone with God. Columbanus is said to have ordered a bear to leave this cave so that he could pray there without distraction. Beside the cave is the holy well, a spring of clear water which the saint is said to have caused to gush forth miraculously to satisfy his faithful servant Domoal. Some of the country people still come to fetch the healing water for the sick.

March 13

PSALM 18:5   GENESIS 35:14–15   PHILIPPIANS 2:17–18

One story told by Jonas describes how Columbanus came to a crowd of pagans gathered in the woods around a vat of beer, which they were offering to Woden. The saint breathed on the cauldron and it burst with a loud noise, so that all the beer poured out on the ground. Jonas must have smiled as he added the comment made by the astounded pagans, that 'the man of God has great strength in his breath'.

March 14

PSALM 26:1   ISAIAH 30:21   ACTS 15:32–41; 16:6–10

The war between the two brothers, King Theuderich of Burgundy (who had persecuted Columbanus) and King Theudebert of Austrasia (his current protector), reached a bloody climax in 612. On the day of the final battle Columbanus, alone in the forest near Bregenz with the monk Chagnoald, had a vision of the slaughter. 'Father,' exclaimed the young monk, 'pray for Theudebert that he may obtain the victory over Theuderich, our common enemy.'

'You give advice that is foolish and contrary to the gospel,' replied Columbanus. 'The Lord asked us to pray for our enemies.'

The death of Theudebert meant that Columbanus' persecutor now added Austrasia, and the German provinces which went along with it, to his former kingdom of Burgundy. Brunhilde set up her court at Metz. Deprived of his protector and once more under the rule of the king and queen who had expelled him, Columbanus now had to face the wrath of the local pagans whom he had previously offended.

Two of his monks were murdered in the woods while they were searching for one of the monastic cows which had been stolen. Other monks recovered their bodies and carried them back to the cloister for burial. Columbanus' first plan seems to have been to traverse the forests of the Allgau and reach the Danube basin. A vision convinced him, however, that he should head for Italy (where he was to found an important monastery at Bobbio) and he announced his decision to the community. Gall, with his knowledge of the Germanic dialects, was reluctant to follow his master.

March 15

PSALM 26:4   JUDGES 7:2–3   MATTHEW 7:13–14

Capable of all tasks, Columbanus set his heart on self-denial. Scholarship had failed to impress its objective balance on the poetic ardour of his nature, and solitude led him to seek truth on the side of the minority. Once entered on a quarrel, his courage never flinched.

Great strength of body matched his strength of mind, and his openness of manner did not belie the beauty of his face. Nonetheless, an abstract devotion to principle tended to blight his warm spirit with the chill of precision. Lacking originality, his talents were best suited to the quiet of the cloister, yet sheer determination made him an outstanding leader of his age.

March 16

PSALM 26:5–7   ECCLESIASTES 2:10–11, 16
      PHILIPPIANS 2:12–16

A gentle warmth of understanding, combined with a fervent faith, caused Columbanus to be credited with strange powers of healing, both of the body and the soul. Remarkable predictions, guided in part by the shrewdness of his political observation, clothed him with the mysterious aura of a seer. Except for the more pedantic type of punning, he was devoid of humour – yet the very tenderness of his natural melancholy rendered him attractive to all classes of society, so the noblemen entrusted him with their sons' education, and kings and courtiers were ready to welcome his reproof.

His character was so complex and so contrary – humble and haughty, harsh and tender, pedantic and impetuous by turns, but its guiding and unifying pattern was the ambition of sainthood. All his activities were subordinate to this one end, and with the self-sacrifice that can seem so close to self-assertion, he worked out his soul's salvation by the one sure pathway that he knew.

At home with everyone, he rested nowhere.

He was a missionary through circumstance; a monk by vocation; a contemplative, too frequently driven to action by the world; a pilgrim, on the road to paradise. 'What then are you, human life?' he wrote. 'You are the road of mortals and not their life, with sin at the beginning and death at the end.'

March 17   Patrick   *Joseph of Arimathea*

PSALM 61:2–5   ECCLESIASTES 11:5–9
I CORINTHIANS 9:26–27

What then are you, human life? You are the road of mortals and not their life, with sin at the beginning and death at the end. You would have been a true life if the sin of man's first transgression hadn't shattered you. Then you became fragile and mortal, and marked all your travellers for death. So you are the road to life, not life itself; you are a real road but not a level one, long for some, short for others, broad for some, narrow for others, joyful for some, sad for others, for all alike fleeting and irrevocable. A road is what you are, a road; but you are not clear to all. Many see you, and few understand you to be a road. For you are so wily and so enticing that few know you as a road. Therefore you are to be questioned but not believed and given bail; you are to be traversed but not inhabited, wretched human life. For no one dwells on a road, but travels it, so that those who walk upon the road may dwell in their homeland.

Why then, mortal life, are you dwelt in, loved and protected by the stupid and the lost, but despised by those with sense and guarded against by those that shall be saved? You have to be feared and shunned a great deal, human life. You are so fleeting, so slippery, so dangerous, so short, so uncertain, that you'll vanish like a shadow or a mirage or a cloud, of nothingness or emptiness. Thus while you are nothing, mortal life, except a road, a mirage, fleeting and void, or a cloud, vague and feeble, and a shadow like a dream, we must journey along you so anxiously, so carefully, so speedily, that all intelligent people should hurry like travellers to their true homeland, sure of the past, but worried by what still remains.

This life is to be considered as a road and an ascent. Let us not seek *en route* what shall be in our homeland. Therefore we must beware lest perhaps we be carefree on the way, and fail to reach our true homeland.

Columbanus

March 18

PSALM 65:5–8   2 CHRONICLES 20:37   MATTHEW 8:23–27

In 613 Columbanus wrote an impassioned letter to Pope Boniface concerning the burning issues of the day:

I'll speak as a friend, disciple, and one who follows in your footsteps, not as a stranger. Therefore I'll speak out freely, and say to those who are our captains and pilots and mystical watches of the spiritual ship: 'Look out, for the sea is stormy and is being lashed by fatal gusts.' It is the tempest of the entire element, surging up everywhere and convulsed on every side, that threatens the mystical vessel with shipwreck. Hence, I, a frightened sailor, dare to scream: 'Look out, for water has already entered the vessel of the Church, and the ship is in peril.'

March 19

PSALM 66:16–20   PROVERBS 29:9   I CORINTHIANS 6:4–8

I can't understand how a Christian can quarrel with a
Christian about the faith. Whatever an orthodox Christian
who rightly glorifies the Lord will say, the other will
answer Amen, because he also loves and believes alike. Let
us therefore all say and think the one thing, so that both
sides may be one – all Christians.

Columbanus

March 20   *Cuthbert   Herebert*

PSALM 68:1–2   2 KINGS 9:22, 30–37   MATTHEW 10:18–20

Back in Gaul, Columbanus was not forgotten. The victorious
Theuderich of Burgundy died in Metz in 613, only half a year
after the murder of the defeated Theudebert. Queen Brunhilde
was captured by the army of Neustria and, having been first
flogged, stripped naked and exhibited on a camel's back for three
days by order of King Clothair, she was tied to the tail of a wild
horse which galloped in various directions until it tore her body to
pieces. Her body was then burned like offal outside the camp.
Jonas notes the triumph of King Clothair as the precise fulfilment
of six prophecies made by Columbanus.

The king himself, now master of nearly all Gaul, sent Abbot
Eustasius of Luxeuil with an escort of noblemen all the way to
Bobbio to invite Columbanus to return to Luxeuil. Columbanus
tactfully declined the invitation, while exhorting Eustasius to be
a good abbot and to seek the king's assistance for Luxeuil. In a
letter to King Clothair, which has not survived, the Irishman
issued some words of rebuke – perhaps taking him to task for the
inhuman degradation of Queen Brunhilde.

Choosing solitude, Columbanus acquired great public influence. Teaching humility, he found himself obliged to correct both
popes and kings. While hot to enter a dispute wherever he
believed that wrong had been committed, his pent-up energies,
like a peal of thunder, quickly cleared the air and he was at once
able to return to the sober calm of common sense. His quick
resentment generally harboured no lingering fires.

March 21

PSALM 69:6   GENESIS 4:9   EPHESIANS 4:25

During his final days on earth, Columbanus' thoughts were on
Gall, the last surviving Irishman of the gallant band who had
accompanied him from Bangor, his constant companion over half
the roads of Europe.

When they had parted, Gall had been ill and insisted on
remaining when Columbanus was directed in a vision to travel
on to Italy. He was commanded under holy obedience never again
to celebrate Communion in Columbanus' lifetime.

On his deathbed, Columbanus ordered that the staff with
which he had trudged through the Vosges and the Jura, the Alps
and the Apennines, should be sent to Gall as a token of forgiveness. Then, in the early hours of Sunday November 23, 615, he
breathed his last.

Hundreds of miles to the north, Gall woke his deacon
Magnoald and told him to prepare everything to celebrate Mass.
He had learned in a vision that his lord and father Columbanus
had passed from the miseries of this life to the joys of paradise
that very day. When the Mass was ended, Magnoald hurried to
Bobbio and found that the vision had been true. He returned bearing the staff.

March 22

PSALM 27:10   JUDGES 14:6   MATTHEW 10:34-39

It is the misfortune of commanding characters to arouse consuming hatreds; and Columbanus, by the outspoken freedom of his mind, was plunged into animated quarrels for the greater portion of his active life. His integrity was hard and cutting as a diamond. Ruthless to himself, he could be inexorable in his demands on others with a determination that not even a mother's tears were able to soften into compromise.

G. S. M. Walker

Jonas tells us that Columbanus' mother had dreamed before he was born that a brilliant sun arose from her breast and illuminated the whole world. Columbanus told his mother he was leaving home. He must break with the family circle for ever and dedicate himself completely to preparation for the life of self-sacrifice that lay ahead. She pleaded with him, burst into tears and threw herself across the threshold to block his exit. He asked her not to grieve, and then in the first of several decisions which to our way of thinking seem so hard and unrelenting, decisions which often appeared cruel and hurtful to his friends, he stepped across her prostrate body and set off for the north, knowing they would never meet again.

March 23 *Ethilwald of Farne Felgild*

PSALM 15:1-5   ISAIAH 58:12   LUKE 19:1-10

If any of the laity sheds blood in a squabble, or wounds or maims his neighbour, he is to be forced to make good the damage he has done. If he has not the wherewithal to pay, let him first carry on his neighbour's work, as long as the latter is sick, and send for the doctor. After the man's recovery, let him do penance for forty days on bread and water. If any layman becomes drunk, or eats and drinks to the point of vomiting, let him do penance for a week on bread and water.

The Penitential of Columbanus

March 24 *Oscar Romero*

PSALM 145:18   MICAH 4:2   COLOSSIANS 3:11–16

Columbanus wrote to the French bishops meeting at Châlons in 603:

Pray for us as we also do for you, wretched though we be, and don't look on us as aliens from you. For we are all fellow members of one body, whether Franks or Britons or Irish or whatever our race. Thus let all our races rejoice in knowledge of the faith and in recognizing the Son of God. Let us all hasten to approach to perfect manhood, to the measure of the age of fullness of Jesus Christ. In Him let us love one another, praise one another, correct one another, encourage one another, pray for one another, so that with Him and with one another we may reign and triumph.

March 25

PSALM 147:1   ISAIAH 40:10–11   ACTS 15:22–29

Columbanus' diplomatic skills are clearly evident in the following letter, which he wrote to the newly elected Pope in 604 or 607 about the divisive question of the date for celebrating Easter:

Give us your opinion; it will be a sweet consolation in our labours. You will thus confirm, if it is not contrary to the faith, the tradition of our predecessors. Thereby we shall be able through your decision to observe in our pilgrimage the rite of Easter as we have received it from our ancestors. For it is clear that we are in our native land as long as we accept no rules of those Franks. We stay in seclusion, harming no one. We abide by the rule of our predecessors. It was to defend these that we wrote both to you, apostolic father, as I have said, and to your brethren, our neighbours and our fathers in Christ, those letters which this note commends to you. We cannot do justice to the merits of the case, as our opponents indulge more in rage than reason. But we now at the opportune moment ask for the vote which your authority can give so that with a decision we may be able to live amongst those men with the peace of church unity. This is what the holy fathers, namely Polycarp and Pope Anicetus, taught – to live without offence to the faith, nay persevering in perfect charity – each retaining what he has received and 'remaining wherein he has been called'.

Farewell, Pope most dear in Christ. Remember us, both in your holy prayers beside the ashes of the saints, and in your most dutiful decisions, following the hundred and fifty authorities of the Council of Constantinople, who decided that churches of God planted in pagan nations should live by their own laws, as they had been taught by their fathers.

March 26

PSALM 142   JOB 23:1–10   EPHESIANS 4:2–6

Letter from Columbanus to Attala, the new abbot of Luxeuil (610):

> You must chiefly strive for peace, 'ever anxious to preserve unity of spirit in the bond of peace'. I'm broken, I confess, for this reason: while I wished to help all, 'when I spoke to

them they fought against me without cause', and while I
trusted all, I don't wish you to undertake so great a task,
under which I sweated; for you know already how tiny was
my knowledge, just a drop. You have learnt that all warn-
ings are not suitable for all, since natures are diverse and
the characters of people differ widely among themselves.
But what am I doing? I'll soon be urging you to that huge
task from which I'm flying myself. If I go on to diversity
of doctrine, I'll stay within bounds. Therefore let you be
many-sided and adaptable to the direction of those who
obey you with faith and love. But you must fear even their
very love, because it will be dangerous to you.

March 27

PSALM 40:8   JEREMIAH 23:3–4   PHILIPPIANS 1:3–14

Letter from Columbanus to the monks of Luxeuil (610):

Examine your consciences, whether you are more pure
and holy in my absence. Don't seek me through love, but
through necessity alone. May you be no poorer by this
event, and don't through this parting seek a freedom that
would make you slaves to the vices. He who loves unity is
mine; he who divides is not mine, for 'he who does not
gather with Me,' says the Lord, 'scatters.'

Moreover, if you see perfection further removed from
you than before, and fate keeps me away from you, and
Attala is not strong enough to govern you, then as your
brethren are here in the neighbourhood of the Britons, unite
yourselves all together in one group, whichever is the
better, that you may more easily fight against the vices and
snares of the devil. Meanwhile let the man whom you all
have elected be over you: because if I'm free to do so, I'll
take care of you, God willing. But if the locality pleases

you and God builds with you there, 'increase to thousands of thousands' there with His blessing.

Pray for me, my own children, that I may live to God.

In another place, Columbanus writes:

Perhaps my own will is not without its attraction; God's will be done in all things. If He will, He knows my desire.

March 28

PSALM 118:22–23   ISAIAH 55:9   MARK 8:38

But what do I care about saving face before anyone, when zeal for the faith needs to be shown? Before God and angels I shall be undaunted; it is praiseworthy to be embarrassed before men for God's sake. If I'm listened to, the gain will be shared; if I'm ignored, God will still reward me.

Columbanus

March 29

PSALM 19:1–4   ISAIAH 26:2   MATTHEW 16:18–19

These are the words of the holy One, the true One, who has the key of David, who opens and no one will shut, who shuts and no one opens: 'I know your works. Look, I have set before you an open door, which no one is able to shut. I know that you have but little power, and yet you have kept My word and have not denied My name. I will make those of the synagogue of Satan who say that they are Jews and are not, but are lying – I will make them come and bow down before your feet, and they will learn that I have loved you.'

Revelation 3:7–9

From Columbanus' letter to Pope Boniface IV in 613:

> If it may be said that you are almost heavenly beings because of Christ's twin apostles (I speak of those whom the Holy Spirit called 'heavens declaring the glory of God' to whom is applied that text: 'their voice to the ends of the earth'), then Rome is also head of the churches of the world, saving the special prerogative of the place of the Lord's resurrection. Thus, as your honour is great in proportion to the dignity of your See, you need to take equally great care not to lose your reputation through some error. Power will rest with you just so long as your principles remain sound. The real key-bearer of the kingdom of Heaven is he who opens up true knowledge to the worthy and shuts to the unworthy. If on the other hand he does the opposite, he will be able neither to open nor shut.

March 30

PSALM 36:6A   JOB 11:7–9   I JOHN 5:7–12

Who then is God? He is Father, Son and Holy Spirit, yet one God. Seek no further concerning God; for those who wish to know the great deep must first study the nature of things. Knowledge of the Trinity is properly compared to the depth of the sea, according to the saying of the Sage: 'And the great deep, who shall discover it?' If then a man wishes to know the deepest ocean of divine understanding, let him first, if he is able, scan that visible sea. The less he finds his knowledge of those creatures which lurk beneath the sea to be, the more he should realize his ignorance of the depths of its Creator, for the one triune God is an ocean that cannot be crossed or explored. High is the heaven, broad the earth, deep the sea and long the ages; but higher and broader and deeper and longer is His knowledge. For

He is extolled by the natural world, He who created it from nothing.

Columbanus

March 31

PSALM 18:28   2 SAMUEL 22:29   MATTHEW 25:1–13

Lord, grant me, I pray You, in the name of Jesus Christ, Your Son, my God, the charity that does not fail, so that my lamp may be always lit, never extinguished, and may burn for me and give light to others.

Columbanus

April

THE BOOK OF THE LAW

April 1 *Mary of Egypt*

PSALM 2:10–12   EXODUS 21:1–6   LUKE 17:7–10

> Thy measure of prayer shall be until thy tears come;
> or thy measure of work or labour till thy tears come;
> or thy measure of work or labour, or of thy genuflections,
> until thy perspiration come often, if thy tears are not free.
> *From the Rule of St Columba of Iona*

April 2

PSALM 4:5–8   EXODUS 23:14–16   LUKE 17:11–17

Remembering to say thank you is important, not just at special feasts and festivals, but in our everyday work and prayer.

Writing about monasticism in Egypt at around 390, Palladius reports:

> Some toiled in garden and field, sowing and tending the vineyards; others worked at building, cutting logs and shaping stones; still others went quietly about the tasks of weaving, cooking and maintaining the machinery of settlement. Then at 3 o'clock each afternoon, one might stand and hear how the strains of psalmody arise from each habitation, so that one believes one is high above the world in paradise. They occupy the church only on Saturday and Sunday.

April 3

PSALM 5:3–12   EXODUS 31:14   LUKE 13:10–17

> Work is not always required. There is such a thing as sacred idleness, the cultivation of which is now fearfully neglected.
>
> *George Macdonald*

The Sabbath is holy to us, set apart for us, not just to honour God, but for our good also.

The Celtic Church seems largely to have observed Saturday as the Sabbath, and broken bread on Sundays in honour of the resurrection of Jesus, but otherwise treating it as a normal working day. Slowly the preference for Sunday observation took root instead.

Each day is a day for prayer, and we should not give up meeting together for worship whenever that may be, but how do we safeguard some kind of Sabbath or day for rest?

Its importance still stands in Scripture, not as an excuse for legalism, but because God has said that it is important for His people.

How then shall *we* live?

April 4 *Martin Luther King Jr*

PSALM 6:5–9   LEVITICUS 5:1   MATTHEW 27:21–24

> I wash my hands in innocence, and go around Your altar, O Lord.
>
> *Psalm 26:6*

> First they came for the Jews
> and I did not speak out
> because I was not a Jew.

Then they came for the Communists
and I did not speak out
because I was not a Communist.
Then they came for the trade unionists
and I did not speak out
because I was not a trade unionist.
Then they came for me
and there was no one left
to speak out for me.

Pastor Martin Niemöller

Am I my brother's keeper?

April 5

PSALM 14:2–3   LEVITICUS 22:21–22   I PETER 1:18–20

O Son of God, do a miracle for me, and change my heart;
Thy having taken flesh to redeem me was more difficult
than to transform my wickedness.

Irish, fifteenth century

O God, and Spirit, and Jesu, the Three,
from the crown of my head, O Trinity,
to the soles of my feet mine offering be;
come I with my name and my witnessing,
come I with my contrite heart, confessing,
come unto Thee, O Jesu my King –
O Jesu, do Thou be my sheltering.

From South Uist

April 6

PSALM 15:1–5   LEVITICUS 24:18–22   MATTHEW 5:38–45

What is this perfect word of love?
Can I confess to You the truth?
– I want an eye for an eye
and a tooth for a tooth.
You tell me, 'Turn the other cheek…'

Love your friends and hate your enemy
– well, that seems reasonable to me.
But You say, 'If that's true, the pagans
do as much as you. My Father lets the
sun rise on the evil and the good.'

Well, here I am again,
knocking at Your door.
You say,
   'Go brother…
      go woman…
         sin no more.'

Ann Liddell

April 7

PSALM 22:12–15   DEUTERONOMY 6:4–5
   I CORINTHIANS 15:30–34

It is the words of Psalm 22 that Jesus calls out from the cross, and He would know them by heart. Like the Celtic saints, young Jews were taught to memorize Psalms. The words would come immediately to Him.

He could not see, could not feel HIM near; and yet it is 'My God' that He cries.

Thus the will of Jesus, in the very moment when His faith seems about to yield, is finally triumphant. It has no feeling now to support it, no beatific vision to absorb it. It stands naked in His soul and tortured, as He stood naked and scourged before Pilate. Pure and simple and surrounded by fire, it declares for God.

George Macdonald

April 8

PSALM 23:3–4   DEUTERONOMY 16:19   LUKE 21:1–4

I have hidden Your word in my heart, so I might not sin against You.

Psalm 119:11

The words of Scripture assume different values from those held by the world around us. They restore a sense of proportion.

Taking bribes is not acceptable; accepting gifts from interested parties distorts the fairness of our perspective, or makes us dubious of our own lack of bias.

Second best is never good enough for God, and all is always more than a little, even when a little is a lot and all is not very much. Little becomes much when you place it in the Master's hands (John 6:5–9).

April 9   *Dietrich Bonhoeffer*

PSALM 25:1–3, 20   DEUTERONOMY 19:4–13   HEBREWS 13:6

The monasticism of the Celts can also be better understood from the standard of Old Testament ways. Modelled on the cities of refuge, the monastery consisted of a walled village in which the mixed society of a Christian community lived lives of virtue and devotion separated from the evils of their heathen neighbours. Hospitality was dispensed. Man and woman and children, single and families, lived under the guidance of a leader who might be a clergyman or layman, and was called an abbot.

Leslie Hardinge

There are differences between the cities of refuge and Christ our refuge. They protected only the innocent. Christ died for the guilty, for the deliberate sinner. He is nearer than any city of refuge. A runner could fail, but someone who looks to Christ can never fail (John 6:37).

Francis A. Schaeffer

April 10

PSALM 31:19   DEUTERONOMY 28:1–19, 23, 45
JAMES 1:22–25

God is present in the blessing. He hems us in behind and before.

You have hemmed me in behind and before, and laid Your hand upon me. If I go up into heaven You are there: if I make my bed in hell still You are there.

Psalm 139:5, 8

Even when our choices mean that we walk into a curse, we find that He has been there too, before us. (Deuteronomy 21:23 says, 'He who is hanged on a tree is accursed of God,' and in Galatians 3:13 Paul explains the meaning of this when he writes, 'Christ has redeemed us from the curse of the law, by being made a curse for us.') Christ is before us, and He gives Himself to reverse the curse. He challenges us to trust in Him.

Son of God,
  be at the outset,
Son of God,
  be surety, friend;
Son of God,
  make straight my way yet,
Son of God,
  at my seeking's end.

From Morar, Western Highlands

DIETRICH BONHOEFFER

These readings are taken from the writings and life of Dietrich Bonhoeffer, who was hanged in Flossenburg concentration camp three weeks before Hitler's suicide and the end of the Second World War. He had studied theology, and before ordination did a student exchange to the USA. There he saw at first hand the evils of racism, little guessing how relevant it would soon become to life in Germany. He was ordained, and lectured at Berlin University where his talk of peace was unpopular; but his heart lay with a confirmation class of 50 boys from a slum estate. The Church was riddled with nationalism, anti-Semitism and compromise. Bonhoeffer withdrew to a Lutheran church in London, but he soon knew he must be back amongst his own people at such a critical time. So he returned and became director of the Confessing Church seminarians, 25 young men whom he tried to raise in community. They dispersed when the Nazis closed the seminary, but secretly studied under Bonhoeffer, assessing the 'cost of discipleship'. The net tightened around the Jews and Bonhoeffer withdrew this time to America, knowing he must return again – as a pacifist and almost certainly to face death. He became a resistance worker, and was part of a failed plot to assassinate Hitler. But it was his evasion of call-up for military service that led to his arrest. He wrote alternately to his parents and fiancée when he was allowed. He supported and prayed for his fellow prisoners. Perhaps he died because of his political convictions and not as a Christian martyr, but Bonhoeffer would say there was no distinction between the two.

April 11

PSALM 5:1–3   EXODUS 24:4–7   MATTHEW 5:38–39

We want to meet Christ in His Word. We turn to the text in our desire to hear what it is that He wants to give us today through His Word. Meet Him first in the day, before you meet other people. Every morning lay upon Him everything that preoccupies you and weighs you down, before new burdens are laid upon you. Ask yourself what still hinders you from following Him completely and let Him take charge of that, before new hindrances are placed in your way. His fellowship, His help, His guidance for the day through His Word – that is the goal. Thus you will begin the day freshly strengthened in your faith.

Meditating on the Word

April 12

PSALM 4:1–4   JOB 2:11–13   MATTHEW 6:22–24

There is a kind of listening with half an ear that presumes already to know what the other person has to say. It is impatient, inattentive listening that despises the brother and is only waiting for a chance to speak and so get rid of the other person. It is little wonder that we are no longer capable of the greatest service of listening that God has committed to us, that of hearing our brother's confession, if we refuse to give ear to our brother on lesser subjects. Christians have forgotten that the ministry of listening has been committed to them by Him who is Himself the great listener and whose work they should share. We should listen with the ears of God that we may speak the words of God.

Life Together

April 13

PSALM 103:20–22   I KINGS 19:15–16, 19–21   MATTHEW 7:1–2

We must be ready to allow ourselves to be interrupted by God. God will be constantly crossing our paths and cancelling our plans by sending us people with claims and petitions. We may pass them by, preoccupied with our more important tasks, as the priest passed by the man who had fallen among thieves, perhaps reading the Bible. When we do that we pass by the visible sign of the cross raised athwart our path to show us that, not our way, but God's way must be done. It is a strange fact that Christians, and even ministers, frequently consider their work so important and urgent that they will allow nothing to disturb them. They think they are doing God a service in this, but actually they are disdaining God's 'crooked yet straight path'. They do not want a life that is crossed and balked. But it is part of the discipline of humility that we must not spare our hand where it can perform a service and that we do not assume that our schedule is our own to manage, but allow it to be arranged by God.

Life Together

April 14

PSALM 34:19   JEREMIAH 15:15, 20   MATTHEW 7:7–11

The answer of the righteous person to the sufferings which the world causes him is to bless. That was the answer of God to the world which nailed Christ to the cross: blessing. God does not repay like with like, and neither should the righteous person. No condemning, no railing, but blessing. The world would have no hope if this were not so. The world lives and has its future by means of the blessing of

God and of the righteous person. Blessing means laying one's hands upon something and saying: 'You belong to God in spite of all.' It is in this way that we respond to the world which causes us such suffering. We do not forsake it, cast it out, despise or condemn it. Instead, we recall it to God, we give it hope, we lay our hands upon it and say: 'God's blessing come upon you; be blessed, you dear God-created world, for you belong to your creator and redeemer.' We have received God's blessing in our happiness and in our suffering. And whoever has been blessed himself cannot help but pass this blessing on to the next one; yes, wherever he is, he must be himself a blessing. The renewal of the world, which seems so impossible, becomes possible in the blessing of God.

Meditating on the Word

April 15

PSALM 81:1-3   LEVITICUS 19:33-34   MATTHEW 7:15-20

When Bonhoeffer was in prison, he kept to the church calendar and observed the feasts. The hymnbook and Bible were his sustenance.

A group of them were being moved about as prisoners from one temporary prison after the other as the Allied armies advanced. In Schönberg, they were in a comparatively comfortable school. It was the Sunday after Easter, and it was suggested that they hold a service of worship. There were both Catholics and Protestants in the group, but that caused no difficulty. Confessional differences had become peripheral in the circumstances of their imprisonment. But there was one difficulty. Wassilev Kokorin, one of their number, the nephew of Molotov, was a convinced communist and therefore 'religionless'. Bonhoeffer judged the solidarity of their suffering more important than the sustenance of Christian fellowship in worship. He could not conduct a religious service which excluded one of their number. It was not possible until Kokorin himself had asked for the service.

Edwin Robertson, Bonhoeffer's Heritage

CELTIC INSIGHT

April 16

PSALM 147:3–5   I KINGS 17:10–16   MATTHEW 25:44–45

> O king of stars!
> whether my house be dark or bright
> never shall it be closed against anyone,
> lest Christ close His house against me.
>
> If there be a guest in your house
> and you conceal aught from him
> 'tis not the guest that will be without it
> but Jesus, Mary's son.

April 17

PSALM 51:6–8   DANIEL 4:34–37   MATTHEW 10:42

Did you ever hear the story of the Fisher King?

It begins with the king as a boy, having to spend the night alone in the forest to prove his courage so he can become king. And while he's spending the night alone he's visited by a sacred vision. Out of the fire appears the Holy Grail, the symbol of God's divine grace.

And a voice said to the boy, 'You shall be keeper of the grail, so that it may heal the hearts of men.' But the boy was blinded by greater visions of a life filled with power and glory and beauty ... and in this state of radical amazement ... he felt for a brief moment not like a boy, but invincible, like God. So he reached into the fire to take the Grail, and the Grail vanished, leaving him with his hand in the fire to be terribly wounded...

...Now as the boy grew older his wound grew deeper until one day life for him lost its reason. He had no faith in any man, not even himself; he couldn't love or feel loved. He was sick with experience. He began to die.

One day a fool wandered into the castle and found the king alone. And, being a fool, he was simple-minded; he didn't see the king. He saw only a man alone and in pain. And he asked the king, 'What ails you?' The king replied, 'I'm thirsty; I need some water to cool my throat.'

So the fool took a cup from beside his bed, filled it with water, and handed it to the king. And as the king began to drink he realized his wound was healed. And he looked at his hands: and there was the Holy Grail, that which he had sought all of his life.

He turned to the fool, and said with amazement, 'How could you find that which my brightest and bravest could not?' The fool replied, 'I don't know. I only knew that you were thirsty.'

As recounted in the film The Fisher King

April 18

PSALM 145:10–12   ISAIAH 40:9–15   ROMANS 10:14

Kenneth MacLeod, in his song 'The Iona Rainbow', has penned verses such as could have been sung by Columba and his monks when putting out to sea:

> O Lord of the heights, whose eye encircles
> the land and the sea, and smiles through the thunder,
> smile on us too, as sail we outward
> to far blue isles, with tales of wonder.
>
> Beyond those waves, strong hearts are longing
> for heaven's own dream, sweet sounds of the Psalter;

fair be our breeze as bear we onward
our Christ and our cross, our song and our altar.

Beside Thy waves our hearts shall praise Thee
for wind and for tide, for share of life's danger;
'tis well if at eve we make our homeland,
'tis well if we sleep the sleep of the stranger.

April 19

PSALM 137:4   GENESIS 9:12–13   JOHN 3:2–3

Columba and his monks envisage the planting of the faith of
Christ in hearts that have known only the teaching of the druids.
The sign of God's promise of faithfulness arches the sky above
their coracles:

Iona shall grow mid far-off oak trees,
the oak trees shall hear of love Thou awakest;
aloft in the sky we see Thy rainbow:
the druid Thou madest, the saint Thou remakest.
                    Kenneth MacLeod, 'The Iona Rainbow'

April 20

PSALM 41:9–10   ISAIAH 58:4–12   ACTS 15:8–12

One of the most contentious issues dividing the Celtic and Roman
traditions of the Church at the time of the Synod of Whitby in 664
was how to calculate the date when Easter should be celebrated.
The outcome of the synod, favourable to the Roman party, had a
major impact on Colman, the bishop of Lindisfarne after whom
this series of readings is named (see Introduction, page xi). In the
paragraph that follows Kate Tristram helps us to understand
the background:

The Jewish Passover was calculated by the moon – by marking the first full moon after the first day of spring. Christians wanted Easter to always be on a Sunday. So Easter was the first Sunday after the first full moon after the first day of spring. The Romans didn't like Easter and Passover coinciding and so wrote tables to avoid this. The Irish had remained with the original way. Hence the conflict. The Romans wanted everyone to submit to the change. The real question was authority. The continental church was becoming more centralized around Rome – this was natural for those who were culturally looking to Rome, because they had done so in the Empire. Northumbria became the battleground. The king at the time, Oswald's brother Oswy, held the synod at Whitby to settle it.

April 21

PSALM 121:6–7   DEUTERONOMY 24:5   ROMANS 15:30–33

JOY INVOCATION
Joy to all those gone before
whose longer stay had pleased us.

Joy to all those left behind
whose leaving would have grieved us.

Joy to all those still to come
whose song may lift the weary.
                    Kenneth MacLeod, 'The Road to the Isles'

TAPESTRY

April 22

PSALM 8:5–8   GENESIS 1:26   REVELATION 4:1–11

> All whom I love into Your safe keeping;
> all that I am into Your tender care.

When God looked at me, long before I ever saw Him, He knew all that I was, all that I might be. He knew me. He saw me.

Me, looking for Jesus, in a desperate, crumbling wreck of life, devastated by divorce, death, lies, cheating. He showed Himself, battered, beaten, dying on a cross. Dying my death, carrying my pain and despair.

He took, I gave: I gave, He took. He took the foundation of all that I was, and smashed it. I asked why I hurt so very much. He said, 'I love you, Steve', over and over again. I lost it all. I was ended, with nothing. When I had nothing, He said, 'I will repay the years the locusts have taken.' The cost of the new design? – the blood of Jesus. I have life, and in abundance. It has been painstakingly built with tender, loving care, to a new design.

For me, my wife and children, Jesus is everything. Coming to that place where He can hold you and you can trust Him, never, ever, to let go, is just so precious. I know His tender, loving care is tenderizing me into the man I must be. All He has given I share with Him. In 1 Peter 5:7 it says, 'Cast all your care on Him, for He cares for you.' I know, I *know* this to be true.

Steve Hartley

April 23

PSALM 19:7–11   GENESIS 1:28–30   REVELATION 7:9–17

> In this attitude of complete dependence, I become
> useful again.

When my daughter began to walk, her steps were faltering and she often fell. She cried and shouted until I ran to pick her up, and she expected me to kiss it better and make everything all right again. As she got better at walking, she was justifiably proud of her achievements, and looked to me for approval and encouragement. Her confidence grew, and she started to toddle further and further from me. Sometimes she walked out of sight and got frightened. Sometimes she fell over. She still called, and I came to make it better. As a Christian, I guess I have been walking rather than toddling for some time. I often run off with great confidence in my own abilities – until I fall over, or get tripped up, or run out of sight of God, and find myself alone with my monsters. Then I am left calling out to God to save me, expecting Him to make it better again. It is right for me to be independent in some things. But how much better for me to know that God is the ground of my being, and that walking with Him is all the security I need! God has given me the world to play and work within, but one day I will stand in heaven before Him, and want to know that I can look Him in the face and say, 'I did what I saw You doing, I went where I saw You going, and I depended on You through it all.'

Dana Beney

April 24

PSALM 30:1–5   ISAIAH 61:1–3   JOHN 20:17

Though the night is here, today I believe.

I believe the most important element in a working faith is that of trust. For me one of the liveliest examples of trust was given by my first wife, who lived with multiple sclerosis for half of her fifty years – and she was in a wheelchair for half of those. May I share with you some words she wrote in the middle of one night. She always fought the wretched disease and wrote about finding a plan for life following her confinement to a wheelchair. It never confined her spirit, and bitterness had no place. She wrote:

> In one sense I've been here before. Ten years ago
> I prayed, got up and walked and lived day by day.
> This time, I prayed and my legs stayed on strike.
> So I work through the quandary of acceptance. As
> always, we have a choice: that between negative
> acceptance – drifting away into nothingness where
> the attitude pertains of 'being done unto', where
> the mind shudders and where 'I' cannot be 'me'.
> This then can lead to anger and bitterness. Or
> there is the choice of acceptance – where you
> take what you have and use it minute by minute,
> recognizing that God is bigger than one's legs and
> providing opportunities where 'I' can still be 'me'.

Later, as she died, she asked me to scatter her ashes on the outgoing tide off the west side of Holy Island, in front of St Cuthbert's Isle. The request and the action had the meaning of giving her back to God with the tide going out and away. As a family we gave her back to God without possession or blame. Our faith does not ask that we do not grieve or mourn; but it does ask that we express the true bond and embrace of eternal love. We know that God is in the night that follows death and that when that night passes, however long it may be, 'joy comes in the morning'.

When I go back to the island to remember and to give thanks, I plant a single flower in the wet sand, within the tide line, so that it will be taken out and away: there is no possession and the spirit is free.

Noel Bevan

A JOURNEY AROUND THE ISLAND OF PILGRIMAGE

The following readings are reflections by Ant and Clare Grimley following a journey around Ireland – a journey away from the expected, towards the eternal mercy and love of the Trinity.

April 25

PSALM 121:5–8   GENESIS 24:42   EPHESIANS 5:15–17

PILGRIMAGE IS A WAY OF LIFE

One of the best-known of the Desert Fathers of fourth-century Egypt, St Sarapion the Sindonite, travelled once on a pilgrimage to Rome. Here he was told of a celebrated recluse, a woman who lived always in one room, never going out. Sceptical about her way of life – for he was a great wanderer – Sarapion called on her and asked, 'Why are you sitting here?' To this she replied, 'I'm not sitting, I am on a journey.'

I am not sitting, I am on a journey. All Christians may apply these words to themselves. To be a Christian is to be a traveller. Our situation, say the Greek Fathers, is like that of the Israelite people in the desert of Sinai. We live in tents, not houses, for spiritually we are on a journey through the inward space of the heart, a journey not measured by the hours of our watch or the days of the calendar, for it is a journey out of time into eternity...

> Christianity is more than a theory about the universe, more than teachings written down on paper; it is a path along which we journey – in the deepest and richest sense, the way of life.

> *Kallistos Ware*

April 26

PSALM 25:5   JOSHUA 21:43–45   ACTS 2:25–26

HOPE IS WHERE THE PILGRIM'S HEART IS

Perhaps a high point in a pilgrimage is when the next place to be visited is a long-awaited one. For us, Skellig Michael (a monastic settlement on a remote, sharp peak of rock eight miles off the County Kerry coast) was such a place. The day began white and misty and our hearts were filled with wonder. We made our way down to the small harbour with plenty of time to spare. Like good little schoolchildren we lined up where the boat left, expectancy on our lips and in the air. But our hearts sank as the weather worsened and the boat was unable to sail. There was no consolation as we retraced our steps, now heavy. Yet the pilgrim must expect disappointments. When I was a child I would have been determined to get what I wanted; now older, I should let things go, knowing they may never return.

When on pilgrimage, routes set in stone may defeat the purpose: I am on a journey without an end, stopping off at I know not where. But my Master knows, and that is enough.

April 27

PSALM 84:5   EXODUS 13:21   LUKE 9:62

THE HEART OF PILGRIMAGE: THE PERPETUAL PREPARATION FOR THE SEA OF LIFE

A curragh is never a finished project: there are always repairs that need to be made and, for long journeys, great preparation is involved. So it is with pilgrimage – and, in consequence, our lives. We need to have our curragh waiting out at sea when our Lord calls. Frail craft bobbing around, totally at the mercy of the elements, is how we are in this world too. As the skin of the curragh begins to tighten and the wooden ribs begin to wear, the boat reflects every journey undertaken. Our hearts, too, reflect every pilgrimage.

> Christians must travel in perpetual pilgrimage as guests of the world.
>
> *Columbanus*

April 28

PSALM 116:16–19   JEREMIAH 1:4–5   GALATIANS 3:26–29

CELTIC SPIRITUALITY: UNCOVERING THE ESSENCE OF MAN

In the middle of a sprawling, dirty town lay the small cathedral of Ardfert, the place where St Brendan had begun a community. Excavations were being undertaken to try and release the original beauty of the monastery that had been built, and built over, by successive generations. The archaeologists were like investigators, deciding what that bit was and why it had been placed there. But all the time they were going deeper – getting to the heart of Ardfert.

When on pilgrimage, fortifications built over our heart need to be investigated too. We need to try to uncover what was originally there. Perhaps the experiences gained on pilgrimage serve only to bring us back to when we were created. We need to renew the fervour of that first building of a holy place on newly claimed ground. We need to honour our King and Creator by being an internal expression of our outward monasteries.

April 29

PSALM 34:20–22   JONAH 1:4–9   JOHN 21:1–6

PILGRIMAGE: LET GOD DO THE ROWING

In the middle of an artificial Celtic settlement at Craggnouwen,

County Clare, lay the biggest challenge to our understanding of pilgrimage. For here was Tim Severin's near-perfect reconstruction of the curragh in which Brendan sailed on his voyage.

Enclosed in a glass pyramid, as if they were afraid it might escape, *Brendan* shouted of long sleepless nights on watch, the burning of ropes on hands, the unwanted facts of days without food and drink. But more than that, it was real – we could touch it, smell it.

St Brendan had sailed away. But we were not sailing in his boat, in his way. *Brendan* proved you could get back to sixth-century simplicity in the twentieth century. But you had to let God do the rowing.

April 30

PSALM 139:7–10   JOB 16:22   PHILIPPIANS 2:16

A RETURN TO ALL THINGS 'OLD'

After finishing a pilgrimage and looking back on it, the feelings we felt, the sights we saw, the successes and failures, begin to feel like old friends. But old friends are easy to forget if you are not careful. And we must be careful to remember our own journey – each individual story along the way. Not so that it is set in concrete or venerated to a place on high: but in the same sense that we are careful to remember the Celtic saints and the Celtic Church.

We are on pilgrimage until our King and Master brings our boat gently to rest in His harbour and leads us quietly up the path of His Father's mountain.

> Blessed is the one whose strength is in You, whose heart is set on pilgrimage.
>
> *Psalm 84:5*

May

GOD ALONE SUFFICES

This month's readings, which draw from *Wisdom of the Spanish Mystics* by Stephen Glissold, provide nuggets of spiritual wisdom from the remarkable flowering of Catholic mysticism in Spain – notably from St Teresa of Avila and St John of the Cross – in the sixteenth century. Though many of the greatest mystics were also much occupied with practical affairs, they were all fired with loving concern for those around them. We see them here in the secret intimacy of their spiritual lives, relating their experiences with unvarnished, and often anguished, honesty, struggling to find words for what is ultimately beyond human power to describe.

Yet their message, in its essentials, is clear enough. It offers no short cut to ultimate truth, nor a recipe for instant enlightenment or spiritual bliss. The mystic sees sanctity as a mountain which has to be climbed. The way is that of self-knowledge, self-denial, the divesting of all earthly attachments, until will and desires are totally absorbed in God.

There must be no more than you and God in the world, for He alone must be all things to you.

May 1

PSALM 25:4–5 DEUTERONOMY 15:12–18 LUKE 14:7–11

St Peter of Alcantara was the founder of the 'barefoot Franciscans'. He used to ask God to teach him the patient obedience of a donkey. Every time I do not behave like a donkey it is worse for me. How does a donkey behave? If it is slandered, it keeps silent; if it is not fed, it keeps silent; if it is forgotten, it keeps silent; it never complains, however much it is beaten or ill-used, because it has a donkey's patience. That is how the servant of God must behave.

I stand before you, Lord, like a donkey.

May 2

PSALM 46:1–3   1 SAMUEL 3:2–10   2 CORINTHIANS 12:9–10

St Teresa of Avila and another nun were spending a night in an empty house which was to be turned into a convent. The nun, thoroughly scared, got it into her head that she was going to die in the night and she asked Teresa what she would do all alone in such a place.

'I will think about that if it should happen,' Teresa replied calmly. 'But in the meantime, sister, let us go to sleep!'

May 3

PSALM 121:7–8   PROVERBS 3:3–4   ROMANS 13:10

Some Moors, who were sitting round a fountain, taunted St John of God about his faith and poured scorn on his belief in miracles.

John, who was a very burly fellow, answered, 'Is it not miracle enough that God constrains me not to throw you into the water?'

May 4

PSALM 104:30–31   DANIEL 6:4–5   ROMANS 12:9–13

St John of the Cross was once accosted in the streets of Granada by a woman who accused him of being the father of the baby she was carrying in her arms.

'Who, then, is its mother?' asked St John.

The woman declared that the mother was of noble birth and lived in Granada.

'And where did she live before coming to Granada?' he asked.

The woman answered that she had lived there all her life.

'And how old is the child?' St John asked.

'One year old,' was the reply.

'Then truly he must be the fruit of some great miracle,' the saint remarked, 'for I have been in this city only a few days.' And he calmly went on his way.

May 5

PSALM 149:4   PROVERBS 16:19   PHILIPPIANS 2:1–4

St Teresa of Avila gave her nuns three precepts:

- ◆ to love one another;
- ◆ detachment from all created things;
- ◆ true humility.

'Though I mention this virtue last,' she wrote, 'it is the chief one and includes all the others.'

May 6

PSALM 6:8–10   JOB 1:21   2 CORINTHIANS 12:7–10

St John of the Cross, bitterly persecuted by his brother friars, wrote:

> If you would come to possess Christ, never seek Him without the cross. Those who pass for the friends of Jesus Christ know little of Him, for we see them going in search of solace rather than of His bitter sufferings. God values your readiness to face suffering and deprivation for love of Him more than all the consolations, spiritual visions and meditations you may have.

May 7

PSALM 119:1–7   PROVERBS 28:27   2 CORINTHIANS 9:6–7

St Toribio, Archbishop of Lima, was so charitable to the poor that he not only gave them the food from his own table, but sometimes the silver dishes on which it was served. This worried his sister, who was in charge of the household, and she would then send a servant to buy back the dishes. One day, when he was out visiting, the archbishop was approached by a distraught mother who begged him to provide a dowry for her daughter so that she could marry. Toribio carried no money on him, but he dismounted and gave the woman his mule, saying, 'Take this and sell it; but quickly, before my sister sees!'

May 8

PSALM 92:1–3   JOB 28:28   MARK 1:35–38

A pious lady, curious to see whether St Rose deserved her reputation, visited her home in expectation of an edifying conversation. She could not conceal her disappointment on finding that Rose refused to be drawn.

'It is better to talk *with* God, rather than *about* Him,' Rose at length remarked, and withdrew to her room to pray.

May 9

PSALM 13:3   PROVERBS 16:1   MATTHEW 6:6

St Mariana of Quito was favoured with visions and other mystical graces which she divulged to no one except her confessor. He, thinking to test her obedience and edify the girl, ordered her to give a full account of them to her young niece. Mariana was greatly distressed, but did as she was told.

The niece, amazed at what she heard, hurried away to write it all down. But on reaching her room she found herself unable to recall a single word. In great confusion she returned to her aunt and asked her to repeat everything she had said.

'Tell my confessor,' Mariana replied with a smile, 'that I have done what he ordered. But it seems that the Lord wants us to keep those secrets to ourselves.'

May 10

PSALM 95:6–7   JOB 42:5–6   LUKE 22:41–42

St Teresa of Avila taught:

> The highest perfection does not consist in feelings or spiritual bliss nor in great ecstasies or visions nor yet in the spirit of prophecy, but in bringing your will into conformity with that of God.

May 11 *Comgall*

PSALM 19:14   PROVERBS 21:1–3   I PETER 5:6–10

Writing of the mystic's difficulty in knowing whether his or her experiences were divinely inspired or not, St Teresa of Avila declared that, so long as they were received with true humility, they can do no harm, even were they to come from the devil; whereas, if humility is absent, they can do no good, even if they come from God.

May 12

PSALM 71:7–8   DEUTERONOMY 4:2–6   I CORINTHIANS 13:1–2

A wise prioress noticed that a lay sister, whom she knew had no true vocation for such things, was claiming to see visions, work miracles and to be favoured with frequent raptures.

The prioress sent for her and said, 'Sister, we don't need you here for your raptures, but for washing the dishes.'

After the lay sister had left the convent, the Inquisition, less merciful than the prioress, pronounced her to be possessed by the devil and threatened her with the stake.

May 13

PSALM 39:4–5   JEREMIAH 10:23   PHILIPPIANS 1:21

The following lines are taken from a poem written by St John of the Cross about the impatience of the soul to see God.

> This life I live in vital strength
> is loss of life unless I win You:
> And thus to die I shall continue
> until in You I live at length.
> Listen (my God!) my life is in You.
> This life I do not want, for I
> am dying that I do not die.

Translated by Roy Campbell

May 14

PSALM 51:10–13   GENESIS 18:1–2   PHILIPPIANS 4:6–7

St Peter of Alcantara, though experiencing many mystical phenomena himself, warned:

Do not seek revelations, marvels or extraordinary things, but rather those things our Lord teaches in his Gospel and which Holy Church declares unto you. The devil often transforms himself into an angel of light in these strange things. Set your affections on your cell and on recollection. Commune within yourself with God. Offer your heart naked to His majesty and place yourself in His hands. Give yourself to prayer and heavenly matters and observe obedience. When you are beset by the noise and turmoil of the world, plunge deep into divine contemplation ... as if, in all creation, there were no other things save God and your own soul.

May 15

PSALM 65:9–13   DEUTERONOMY 6:5   MATTHEW 15:31

Master Ramon taught:

When you hear men speak great things, or listen to the singing of the minstrels, or the sound of the wind in the trees, or of the waves breaking on the shore – then love God all the more because of it.

May 16   *Brendan*

PSALM 42:1–3   JOB 37:1–2   I THESSALONIANS 5:15–22

St Alonso told his confessor:

It has sometimes happened that, before going to bed, I have begun praying and continued to do so while at the same time I was really fast asleep. And when I fall asleep as I am praying, I pray in exactly the same way in my sleep as I do when I am awake. I sleep, but my heart keeps watch.

May 17

PSALM 51:3–4   JOB 40:11–12   2 CORINTHIANS 13:5–6

St Teresa of Avila was once driven back to her convent in a carriage belonging to a great lady she had been visiting.

A friar who was an enemy of her reforms began abusing her as she got out: 'So you're the "saint" who is taking everybody in – and going about in a carriage, too!'

The nuns were scandalized, but St Teresa listened to him meekly and remarked: 'He is the only one with the courage to tell me my faults!'

And from that day, no one could persuade her to travel in anything but the poorest and most uncomfortable of carts.

May 18

PSALM 115:14–15   I KINGS 3:5–9   ROMANS 11:33

Answering those who said it was spiritual pride and presumption to try to practise the higher forms of prayer and to strive after perfection, the Abbot of Montserrat put the following question to them:

'Suppose a king has a mind to promote one of his kitchen servants to be steward, as he thinks him well fitted for this, but the servant begs to be excused because he likes working in the kitchen and eating the good food there, or because he is lazy, or afraid of taking responsibility – would he not be much to blame?'

In the same way, a Christian who holds back from the call to follow a more excellent way of life on the plea of humility is guilty of lacking real fervour and conviction.

May 19

PSALM 106:4–5   EXODUS 4:1–5   I PETER 4:10–11

St Alonso taught that, if God chooses to work through us, we should not think that it indicates any merit on our part. With a stick as His instrument, God can work wonders; nor is the stick anything other than a stick because of this. This is what God did with Moses' rod.

May 20

PSALM 32:8   ZEPHANIAH 1:7   I JOHN 3:2–3

Friar Juan Falconi described what came to be called the 'Prayer of Simple Regard':

> To walk with our gaze fixed firmly on God. To contemplate Christ is to look on Him simply with the eyes of faith, without asking oneself or imagining anything further, but just to go on looking at Him, believing in Him and loving Him.

There are no rules or methods. We must simply place ourselves in the presence of God and remain there, resigning ourselves into His hands to do with us whatever He will. We shall soon find that there is little we need to do or understand, and little cause to fear being led astray.

May 21

PSALM 51:1–2   I SAMUEL 24:1–6   HEBREWS 4:12–13

St Teresa of Avila used to say:

> Be gentle with others, but stern towards yourself.

May 22

PSALM 14:5–7   DEUTERONOMY 33:12   PHILIPPIANS 1:29

St Teresa of Avila, when young, venerated a pious old woman
whom she once asked: 'Do you not long to die, Mother? I do; I
am so eager to see my Bridegroom!'

'Not at all, my daughter,' the old woman replied. 'I want to
live as long as I can, so that I may go on suffering for Him. This
won't be possible after my death; there will be plenty of time to
enjoy being with Him then.'

May 23

PSALM 37:7–9   DEUTERONOMY 33:26–27   MARK 14:22–26

Sister Ana Maria, prioress of a Franciscan convent, would find
herself transported into ecstasy while she was preparing to
receive the sacrament of Holy Communion. She wrote:

> I felt the presence of my God beside me, and He said:
> 'Embrace Me! Tomorrow you are to receive Me, and will
> you not now embrace Me?' As He said this, I felt myself
> caught up in God's embrace and filled with majesty,
> grandeur and union with Him, and such great blessings that
> it seemed to me that there was nothing further to be desired
> on earth. This union lasted many days and brought with it a
> great suspension of powers and a loving gratitude which
> permeated all my senses. To be caught up in God's embrace
> and to be made aware of His presence was something per-
> ceived inwardly, not with the eyes of the body. With it there
> came an inner understanding, though my senses were fully
> conscious of it too. And once I had entered into this state, I
> lost the very memory of how I had reached it and any wish
> to leave it again.

May 24

PSALM 22:1–3   ISAIAH 40:7   MARK 15:33–37

When St Teresa of Avila learned that St John of the Cross had
been imprisoned, she commented:

> It is terrible what treatment God allows His friends to
> suffer. But then we should not really complain, for that is
> how He treated His own Son.

May 25

PSALM 5:11–12   DEUTERONOMY 8:3   MARK 10:13–16

St John of the Cross taught:

> Do not imagine that because someone seems not to excel in
> the virtues you think he should have, he is not precious
> in God's sight on account of the things you have not
> thought of.

May 26 *Bede*

PSALM 22:9–10   ISAIAH 49:15–18   JOHN 20:19

Luis de Leon, returning to his university after five years' imprisonment by the Inquisition, resumed his lectures with the words:

> As we were saying yesterday…

May 27

PSALM 77:1 JONAH 2:7 I PETER 4:1-2

St John of the Cross once had a vision in which Christ appeared to him and asked him what favour he wished to be granted.

'Lord, that You may send me trials to suffer for Your sake, and that I may be despised and held of no account,' he replied.

St John died not long afterwards, in disgrace with his Order and in the custody of unfriendly friars.

May 28

PSALM 94:12 JOB 13:1 I JOHN 4:1-2

St John of Avila, known as the Apostle of Andalusia and famous for his skill in the discernment of spirits, proposed some useful yardsticks for testing the authenticity of mystical experiences and revelations:

- Were they in agreement with the teaching of the Scriptures and the Church?
- Were those who received them sure that they were quite free from treachery, since 'the devil can slip in a lie between a thousand truths'?
- Did they help the visionary to lead a more virtuous, truly Christian life, or simply make him talk continuously about them?
- Did the vision leave behind a sense of serenity or merely excitement and curiosity?
- Did it make for deeper humility, with the knowledge that God should favour unworthy sinners with such things, or did it encourage the belief that those so favoured must be something special?

The answers to such questions should help to show whether the visions and revelations stemmed from God or the devil.

May 29

PSALM 145:14-16   I SAMUEL 22:1-3   MATTHEW 6:2-4

St John of God was advised by his friends to go to a city where the king was holding court, in order to beg alms for his hospital. He did so and many people gave generously. But after a few months, he left empty handed.

'I found even more folk there in need of help,' he explained. 'Charity is to be practised wherever you are.'

May 30

PSALM 25:8-11   ISAIAH 57:15   I TIMOTHY 2:14-15

St John of God used to go through the streets of Granada and collect the sick and destitute people he found there. The Archbishop sent for him and told him that he ought to send away the good-for-nothings who were giving his hospital a bad name.

The saint, who had once led a roving life himself, answered respectfully: 'My lord, I know of only one man in my hospital who answers to that description, and that is the sinner, John of God.'

May 31

PSALM 1:1-2   PROVERBS 20:12   ROMANS 12:3

A nun once asked St John of the Cross whether he composed his verses when he was in a state of ecstasy.

'Sometimes God gave them to me,' he replied, 'and at other times I sought them out for myself.'

June

ANTONY OF EGYPT

It was about 285 when Antony went into the Egyptian desert to live in complete solitude. His reputation was such that others were drawn to settle near him. Around 305 he came out of the hermitage to act as their spiritual father, or Abba. Five years later he retired again into solitude. He is often looked upon as the founder of monasticism. Athanasius' *Life of Antony*, which was written shortly after Antony's death, had considerable influence for hundreds of years, inspiring others to imitate Antony's life as a hermit and soldier for Christ.

All the quotations in these readings are from Athanasius' record of Antony's life – except for the last three days, which are from *The Sayings of the Desert Fathers*. Athanasius' words have also been worked into the linking commentary so that the readings as a whole retain as much as possible of the original style (including the practice in Gregg's translation of highlighting in italics any direct quotations from Scripture).

At first, Athanasius' language is startling: so much mention is made of demons and temptations that it could seem an unhealthy preoccupation. It is important to remember that these early monastic writings are set in the context of the individual's struggle to remain faithful and persevere in a dedicated life of simplicity and prayer. Any threatening circumstance or discouraging thought is therefore regarded as the work of the enemy (the devil or his demons). This is particularly so when the thoughts or temptations assaulting a newcomer follow patterns familiar to all who have managed to persevere in prayer in the depths of the desert. Reprisals were only to be expected: the hermit who makes seeking God for His own sake and living for Him the priority of their life is seen as a warrior assailing the forces of evil, and as such a threat to the kingdom of darkness. To speak in this way of enemy assault did not imply that, just because someone is having to deal with temptation, struggle or sin, they are demon possessed!

Instead, these desert-dwellers recognized that progress in the Spirit involves sifting through our thoughts and decisions, lest we unwittingly co-operate with intrusive thoughts which tend only to steal, kill and destroy our solid joys and lasting treasure.

June 1

PSALM 89:11   I CHRONICLES 29:10–14   ACTS 4:32–37

Antony's parents died when he was 18 or 20, leaving him to care for his younger sister. About six months after their deaths, he was on his way to church as usual, thinking about how the apostles had forsaken everything to follow Christ and how in Acts some had sold their possessions and brought the money to the apostles for distribution among the needy. In church that day the Gospel reading happened to be from Matthew 19:21,

> ...and he heard the Lord saying to the rich man, *If you would be perfect, go, sell what you possess and give to the poor, and you will have treasure in heaven.* It was as if by God's design he held the saints in his recollection, and as if the passage were read on his account. Immediately Antony went out from the Lord's house and gave to the townspeople the possessions and land he had from his forebears, so that they would not disturb him or his sister in the least. And selling the rest that was portable, when he collected sufficient money, he donated it to the poor, keeping a few things for his sister.

Lord, when You challenge me from Your Word, make me quick to respond.

June 2

PSALM 68:19   PROVERBS 27:1   COLOSSIANS 3:15-16

When Antony was next in church, he heard the words *Do not worry about tomorrow* from Matthew 6:34 being read. He could not remain any longer, but going out he gave those remaining possessions also to the needy. He placed his sister in the care of nuns and devoted himself to the monastic discipline. There were no monasteries in Egypt at that time, Athanasius tells us, so he lived in isolation not far from his own village. When he heard about an old man who had lived the solitary life from his youth, Antony went to see him and sought to emulate his goodness. In fact, if he heard of some zealous person anywhere, he searched them out like the wise bee, gathering all he could to help him on the road to virtue. All his desire and energy went into his new discipline. He learned how to weigh his thoughts, let go of the past, work to provide himself with food (he gave any money left over to those in need) and, as the work was very repetitive, he learned that he was able to pray constantly.

Athanasius sums up Antony's new way of life by saying that he 'paid such close attention to what was read that nothing from Scripture did he fail to take in – rather he grasped everything, and in him the memory took the place of books'.

Lord, please help me live the life You have called me to with all my heart and energy.

June 3   Kevin

PSALM 109:29-31   JOB 12:16   2 CORINTHIANS 2:11B

Athanasius says the devil could not bear Antony's singleness of heart and set to work against him. He tried to tempt Antony away from his new discipline by reminding him of the possessions he had renounced, of the sister he had left behind, of how good it had been to have money, good food and so on. He pointed out what hard work this new life of virtue was, how weak Antony was and how long a job it would be. Our spiritual enemy will do all he can to throw us off our righteous course, clouding our minds with all kinds of memories, thoughts and worries, but Antony defeated him with strong resolve, great faith and constant prayer.

As the battle grew more severe, we are told that the devil

> advanced against the youth, noisily disturbing him by night, and so troubling him in the daytime that even those who watched were aware of the bout that occupied them both. The one hurled foul thoughts and the other overturned them through his prayers; the former resorted to titillation, but the latter, seeming to blush, fortified the body with faith and with prayers and fasting. And the beleaguered devil undertook one night to assume the form of a woman and to imitate her every gesture, solely in order that he might beguile Antony. But in thinking about Christ and considering the excellence won through Him ... Antony extinguished the fire of his opponent's deception.

In a final showdown, the devil revealed himself to Antony, who sent him fleeing, saying, 'From now on you cause me no anxiety, *for the Lord is my helper, and I shall look down on my enemies*' (Psalm 118:7).

Lord, help me hold tightly to You when I am tempted and so discover how tightly You hold on to me.

June 4 *Eadfrith*

PSALM 18:46–49   DANIEL 3:17   HEBREWS 7:24–25

The battle was won, but the war was not over. Temptation will be with us all to the day we die, and so Antony learned to be vigilant and ready for the enemy's attacks. Antony, now about 35, went to stay in one of the tombs some distance from his village, asking a friend to bring him bread occasionally. Athanasius tells us that, as the door of the tomb closed behind him, the enemy was worried that Antony would soon fill the desert with monks practising this new discipline. So the devil and a multitude of demons set about Antony with such severity that he was left for dead. But by God's providence, for the Lord does not overlook those who place their hope in Him, the friend came the next day to bring him the loaves. Finding Antony lying there, the friend carried him back to the village church, where neighbours and relatives gathered to mourn the saint's death. At around midnight, however, Antony came to his senses and wakened. As he saw everyone sleeping, and only his friend keeping watch, he beckoned to him and asked him to lift him again and carry him to the tombs, waking no one.

Lord, whatever is going on in my life, please help me always to place my trust in You.

June 5

PSALM 27:1–5   DEUTERONOMY 33:29   ROMANS 8:37–39

Alone once again in the tomb and too weak to stand, Antony lay there alone, praying. After the prayer he yelled out:

> Here I am – Antony! I do not run from your blows, for even if you give me more, nothing shall separate me from the love of Christ.

Then he also sang,

> Though an army should set itself in array against me, my
> heart shall not be afraid.

Seeing the need to change tactics, the devil now filled the tomb
with crashing noises as the walls collapsed and the forms of wild
beasts appeared to attack and wound Antony. Despite his pain,
Antony mocked the demons, saying:

> If there were some power among you, it would have been
> enough for only one of you to come. But since the Lord has
> broken your strength, you attempt to terrify me by any
> means with the mob; it is a mark of your weakness that you
> mimic the shapes of irrational beasts … For faith in our
> Lord is for us a seal and a wall of protection.

A divine vision of light then broke into the tomb, restoring its
walls, dispelling the demons and healing Antony's body. Antony
cried out, 'Where were You? Why didn't You appear in the beginning, so that You could stop my distresses?' A voice replied, 'I
was here, Antony, but I waited to watch your struggle. And now,
since you persevered and were not defeated, I will be your Helper
forever, and I will make you famous everywhere.' Immediately
Antony stood and prayed, and he was so strengthened that he felt
his body contained more might than before.

**Lord, please help me to understand that You are with me
always in the midst of trials.**

June 6

PSALM 27:10–12   JOB 1:7   I PETER 5:8–9

An important part of the monastic discipline has always been to discern things for what they are. So when Antony now headed deeper into the desert, zealous to do battle with the devil, he had a vision of a large silver plate on the path. Knowing the wiles of the evil one, he at once saw it as a trick to distract him from his devotion to God; after all, it was ridiculous to suppose that anyone should not have noticed the loss of such a large and precious thing. 'Devil! Take this with you to destruction!' he said, and immediately it vanished like smoke from a fire. Next he saw not an illusion but actual gold on the path, but this time he just rushed past it. As we learn the devil's tricks and deceits, we learn also how to avoid them affecting us.

Arriving at a deserted fort where he would spend the next 20 years, he barricaded himself in, received bread only twice a year, and there continued his life of discipline. He would see no one, and visitors choosing to spend the night outside would hear shouts and cries from within as the demons shouted, 'Get away from what is ours! What do you have to do with the desert? You cannot endure our treachery!' In those days it was understood that the desert was a place where demons particularly dwelt. When those outside were frightened and called out to Antony inside, he would urge them to leave and not to be afraid, telling them to seal themselves with the sign of the cross, depart with confidence and leave the demons to mock themselves.

When some of his friends finally came and tore down the fortress door, Antony came forth as though from a shrine, having been led into divine mysteries and inspired by God. He emerged physically unharmed, pure in soul and utterly balanced in character.

Lord, thank You that when I depend on You and do battle against the evil I find in my life, You keep me from all harm eternally and bring me to maturity in Christ.

June 7

PSALM 27:13–14   ISAIAH 40:28–31   2 THESSALONIANS 3:13

> Jesus said to His disciples, 'Therefore I tell you, do not
> worry about your life, what you will eat, or about your
> body, what you will wear. For life is more than food, and
> the body more than clothing.'
>
> *Luke 12:22–23*

When all the monks came to him for advice one day, Antony told
them to hold on to their eagerness and not to give up or grow
weary of the new life they had begun. Each day, he said, should
be like a fresh start, and so he encouraged them to increase their
dedication, since, after all, this life is so short compared to eternal
life. 'Therefore, my children, let us not lose heart. Let us not think
that the time is too long or what we do is great, *for the sufferings
of this present time are not worth comparing with the glory that is
to be revealed to us*' (Romans 8:18). Whatever we have given up
is as nothing compared to the kingdom of heaven, so what is the
point in yearning to possess anything now? 'Why not rather own
those things that we are able to take away with us – such things as
prudence, justice, temperance, courage, understanding, love, concern for the poor, faith in Christ, freedom from anger, hospitality?'

**Lord, please help me to keep my focus on heaven and the kind
of things You value.**

June 8

PSALM 10:12   MICAH 5:9   COLOSSIANS 2:13–15

Antony says that God created all things good, but that the demons
fell from heaven and do not want Christians to get there, so they
frustrate our journey into heaven. 'Therefore much prayer and

asceticism is needed so that one who receives through the Spirit the gift of discrimination of spirits might be able to recognize their traits – for example, which of them are less wicked, and which more; and in what kind of pursuit each of them exerts himself, and how each of them is overturned and expelled ... *We are not ignorant of his designs* (2 Corinthians 2:11) and ... we ought to set each other on the right path, away from them.' The demons, Antony says, put stumbling blocks in our way in the form of evil thoughts, especially when they see we are progressing well. But, he says, 'we need not fear their suggestions, for by prayers and fasting and by faith in the Lord they are brought down immediately.' Though the assaults and deceptions will continue and take different forms, 'there is no need for us, the faithful, to fear the devil's manifestations nor to worry about his words, for he lies – he speaks no truth whatever ... it is not necessary to fear the demons, for by the grace of Christ all their pursuits come to nothing.'

Lord, praise You that victory is ours in You, and that You are Sovereign over all!

June 9 *Columba*

PSALM 119:137–144   ISAIAH 28:11–13   LUKE 4:5–8

One of the pitfalls into which the early monks could easily fall was excessive zeal. Eager to excel, often more from a desire to compete than to get close to God, they could slip into excessive fasts or vigils, for example. Antony warns that the demons, much as when Christ was tempted in the wilderness, can incessantly recite Scripture, sing hymns, awaken the monk to prayer and so on. They do this to wear down the monk and destroy him. After all, it sounds so devout, how can it be wrong? Antony says:

Nevertheless it is unnecessary to heed them, even if they awaken you for prayer, or counsel you to eat nothing at all, or pretend to level accusations and reproaches concerning actions for which, at another time, they excused us. They do not do these things for the sake of piety or truth, but so that they might bring the simple to despair, and declare the discipline useless, and make men sick of the solitary life as something burdensome and very oppressive, and trip up those who, opposing them, lead it.

There are sometimes demands made on our spiritual lives that do not come from the Lord. Maybe they come from us, maybe somewhere else, but we should not heed them. Rather, Antony says, we should 'devote ourselves to our own purpose in the discipline'. We must not fear these demons, 'even though they seem to assault us or threaten us with death, for they are weak and have power to do nothing except hurl threats'.

Lord, help me to live as You and You alone direct.

June 10

PSALM 46:1–2   NAHUM 1:2   MARK 5:1–13

Since the Lord made His sojourn with us, the enemy is fallen and his powers have diminished. For this reason, though he is able to do nothing, nevertheless like a tyrant fallen from power he does not remain quiet, but issues threats, even if they are only words. Let every one of you consider this, and each will be empowered to treat the demons with contempt.

While we cannot hide from our spiritual enemy as we might from a physical enemy, nevertheless in Christ this enemy has no strength and all he can do is issue threats. If his forces had the power, they would do away with Christians immediately, but they have no such power and the demons, unable to effect anything, play parts as if they were on stage, changing their forms and striking fear in children by the illusion of the hordes and their shapes. For these antics they deserve instead to be ridiculed as weaklings.

Lord, please keep me from being needlessly afraid; help me to live in the power of Your victory won on the cross.

June 11

PSALM 5:8–10   ISAIAH 8:20   JOHN 8:44

> Do not quench the Spirit. Do not despise the words of prophets, but test everything; hold fast to what is good; abstain from every sort of evil.
>
> *1 Thessalonians 5:19–22*

The demons, being part of the created order, are incapable of creating anything new, but they are great mimics, not least of spiritual gifts. Antony warns that we should not be won over when they pretend to prophesy. He says that they often know the future – for instance, that a given person is about to visit us. But 'the demons do this not out of any concern for their hearers, but in order to persuade them to trust them and after that, having brought them under control, to destroy them.' All they are doing is running ahead with the news, he says. It is not so much fore-knowledge as observation – they simply saw the forthcoming visitor set out from home! We are not judged for what we do or do not know, he says, but each of us faces judgement as to whether we have kept the faith and sincerely observed the commandments.

Lord, please help me to test everything and seek Your genuine voice alone.

June 12

PSALM 7:9   ZEPHANIAH 3:13–15   I JOHN 4:18A

Antony warns us that, though the demons will sometimes commend our spiritual discipline (doubtless encouraging pride), we should ignore them. Instead he recommends signing ourselves and our homes with the sign of the cross and praying, so that they will then quickly go – for they cannot bear prayer. The truth is, they are cowards, and they are utterly terrified by the sign of the Lord's cross, because through the power of the cross the Saviour stripped them of their armour and made an example of them. Do not fear them, just pray and pay them no attention. The Lord gives us the ability to discern good and evil and He will bring such tranquillity and gentleness that joy immediately enters the soul, and so does delight, and courage, for the Lord who is our joy, the power of God the Father, is our Companion. Our spiritual enemy disturbs our minds and spirits, causing dejection and despair; yet, when angels appear to believers in Scripture, they always bid them not to fear. So, then, 'if the fear is instantly removed, and its place is taken by unspeakable joy and cheerfulness, confidence and renewed strength, calmness of thought and bravery and love of God, be of good courage and say your prayers. For the joy and the stability of the soul attest to the holiness of the One who is in your presence.' Antony tells us that it is also important not to invent fears for ourselves by entertaining thoughts of how the powers of evil might overcome us. Too often, even today, we are in danger of crediting the evil one with so much power that we can lose heart and hope.

Lord, help me to live in the victory of Your cross.

June 13

PSALM 71:5–8   PROVERBS 3:5–7   COLOSSIANS 3:17

When the Roman Emperor Maximin, who reigned from 305 to 308, began to persecute the Church, he preferred to send Christians down the mines rather than execute them. Antony set out for Alexandria, longing to become a martyr himself, but ended up enthusiastically encouraging those Christians put on trial, and standing with them in their sufferings. He and his companions proved to be so fearless before the court that the judge issued an order that none of the monks was to appear in the law court, nor were they to stay in the city at all. Athanasius tells us how the Lord protected Antony so that others could benefit from what he had learned about how to serve the Lord and grow closer to Him, and how, through his conduct, many were inspired to imitate his way of life. Often, in our deep desire to make some sacrifice for the Lord, we fail to see the value of what we are already doing for Him.

Lord, please protect me from myself and help me to understand what You want of me.

June 14

PSALM 34:1–8   JONAH 2:2   JOHN 14:12–14

On one occasion when Antony sought complete solitude, an army officer called Martinianus became a nuisance to him. His daughter was disturbed by a demon and the distressed father kept knocking at Antony's door and calling on him to pray. Without coming outside, Antony eventually asked this officer why he was calling out to another man: if Martinianus believed in Christ, he could pray just as easily himself and have his prayers answered. Immediately the officer departed, believing and calling on Christ, and having his daughter purified of the demon in consequence.

Lord, when we are in need it is good to have brothers and sisters who will stand with us in prayer, but help us to remember that we need to pray too; we need to knock on Your door as well as on everyone else's.

June 15

PSALM 55:6–8   JEREMIAH 9:1–2   MARK 6:30–34

So many people were now beginning to visit and disturb Antony, that he set out deeper into the desert, to the Thebaid, where no one knew him. As he waited by the river for a boat, a voice came from heaven saying, 'Antony, where are you going, and why?' Antony was quite used to this kind of thing and said he was trying to escape the constant annoyance of people visiting him and asking him to do things that were beyond his power. The voice did not challenge him about this attitude, as we might perhaps have expected, but instead advised, 'Even if you go into the Thebaid, and even if, as you are contemplating, you go down to the pastures in the Nile Delta, you will have more, even twice as much toil to endure. If you truly desire to be alone, go now instead into the inner mountain.'

When he got there three days later, we are told that Antony, as if stirred by God, fell in love with the place, for this was the place the One who had spoken with him at the river bank had designated. Antony made his home there and lived in solitude.

Lord, when I am where you want me to be, I find peace. Please help me to find that place.

June 16

PSALM 61:1–4 PROVERBS 18:10 EPHESIANS 6:10–13, 16–18

Now an old man alone in the inner mountain, Antony devoted himself to prayer and discipline. Those who did find him discovered that he was still wrestling with the demons. Our struggle against temptation and evil will last our whole natural life.

> But they also observed him struggling as if against things visible, and praying against them; and he encouraged the ones who came to him, while at the same time he fought, kneeling and praying to the Lord. And it was truly amazing that being alone in such a desert he was neither distracted by the demons who confronted him, nor was he frightened of their ferocity when so many four-legged beasts and reptiles were there. But truly he was one who, as Scripture says, *having trusted in the Lord*, was *like Mount Sion* (Psalm 125:1), keeping his mind unshaken and unruffled; so instead the demons fled and the wild beasts made peace with him.

When the wild beasts did try to attack, he said to them, 'If you have received authority over me, I am prepared to be devoured by you. But if you were sent by demons, waste no time in retreating, for I am a servant of Christ.' At these words the beasts would flee.

Lord, please help me to place all my trust and confidence in You, for I am also Your servant.

June 17

PSALM 107:4–6, 35   GENESIS 21:14–19   ACTS 15:36

On one occasion some monks came to ask Antony to oversee them for a while. They loaded a camel with bread and water, and set off across the desert. When the heat became oppressive, the water ran out and they could find no more. Despairing for their lives, they let the camel go and lay down to die. This distressed Antony, so he went off a short distance and knelt to pray and immediately the Lord made water gush forth from where he was praying. The monks drank their fill, filled their waterskins and went in search of the camel, which they found with its rope caught round a rock. Then they completed their journey safely.

> And as if bringing provisions from the mountain, he enter-
> tained them with his words, and lent his assistance. Once
> again there was joy in the mountains, and zeal for progress,
> along with the encouragement due to their common faith.

Antony then was full of joy, seeing the ardour of the monks, and seeing also that his sister had come at last to old age still embracing the celibate life of a virgin, and had herself guided others in pursuit of a consecrated life.

Lord, thank You for blessing me with Your provision and protection in times of need. Please help me to be a blessing to others.

June 18

PSALM 19:12–14   ECCLESIASTES 7:9   EPHESIANS 4:26–27

Antony especially urged the monks to:

practise constantly the word of the Apostle, *Do not let the sun go down on your anger* (Ephesians 4:26), and to consider that this had been spoken with every commandment in mind – so that the sun should set neither on anger nor on any other sin of ours. He continued: 'For it is good, even urgent, that the sun should not condemn us for an evil of the day, nor the moon for a sin, or even for an inclination, of the night. That this might be preserved in us, it is good to hear and obey the Apostle, for he says, "Examine yourselves and test yourselves". Now daily let each one recount to himself his actions for the day and night, and if he sinned, let him stop. But if he has not sinned, let him avoid boasting; rather, let him persist in the good, and not become careless, nor condemnatory of a neighbour, nor declare himself righteous *until*, as the blessed apostle Paul said, *the Lord comes who* searches out *the hidden things*' (1 Corinthians 4:5 and Romans 2:16).

Lord, please help me to settle accounts with You each day.

June 19

PSALM 16:7–8   PROVERBS 19:20   MATTHEW 26:36–39

Antony tells us to remember that the Lord knows all our thoughts and actions. Let us then, he says, 'examine ourselves ... and those things we are lacking let us hurry to complete. As a precaution so that we might not sin, let each one of us note and record our actions and the stirrings of our souls as though we were going to give an account to each other.' It was the practice of each of these early monks to find a senior and more experienced monk to whom they could confess their thoughts and struggles, thus disarming the power of evil thoughts and temptations. It is this kind of transparency with another, to whom we make ourselves vulnerable and accountable, that opens the way for spiritual growth and the overcoming of sin and the enemy's deceits. It helps us as we strive for purity of heart and the kingdom of God. We find Jesus being this transparent with Peter, James and John about His own struggles.

Lord, please help me to find sound fellow believers with whom I can be transparent and honest about my own struggles.

June 20

PSALM 103:1–5   EXODUS 15:26   ACTS 14:8–15

Antony taught those he encouraged, and prayed for those who suffered, with whom he sympathized. His prayers for them were frequently answered; yet he was neither boastful when he was heeded, nor disgruntled when he was not. Rather, he gave thanks to the Lord always. He encouraged those who suffered to have patience and to know that healing belonged neither to him nor to mankind at all, but only to God. Therefore, whoever was suffering received the words of the old man as healing and learned not to dwell on their infirmities, but to be patient. Those who were cured were taught not to give thanks to Antony, but to God alone.

Lord, teach me to pray for and stand by my brothers and sisters, ever rejoicing, grateful and patient, always giving glory to You for Your goodness.

June 21

PSALM 16:9–11   PROVERBS 3:21–26   JOHN 10:4

Once Antony had a conversation with someone who visited him, about the soul's passing from this life and where it will be after this.

The next night someone called to him from above, saying, 'Antony, get up – go out and look!' Going out, therefore (for he knew Whom he would benefit from obeying), and looking up he saw someone huge, and ugly and fearsome, standing and reaching to the clouds – and certain beings ascending as if they had wings. And the huge figure extended his hands, and some were being held back by him, but others, flying upwards and finally passing him by, ascended without anxiety. That great one gnashed his teeth over those latter, but over those who fell back he rejoiced. And immediately a voice came to Antony: 'Understand what you have seen!' And his understanding was opened, and he comprehended that it was the passage of the souls, and that the huge figure was the enemy who envies the faithful. And he perceived that he seizes and prevents the passing of those who are under his authority, but he is incapable of seizing, as they pass upwards, those who did not submit to him.

The monks used to talk a lot about how we are never made to sin, only incited to sin. It is up to us, relying on Christ's help, whether or not we consent to our thoughts and the temptations that present themselves.

Lord, help me to place myself under Your authority and to rely on Your Spirit's help to resist evil, sin, deceit and despair.

June 22

PSALM 51:12   PROVERBS 9:8–10   ROMANS 12:2

Often Antony would raise questions and ask to hear from those with him. He always acknowledged that he was helped if someone said anything useful. His face had a great and marvellous grace, and this spiritual favour he had from the Saviour.

Athanasius says that what set Antony apart were such characteristics as the stability of his character and the purity and joy of his soul, which were reflected in his face and demeanour. He tells us that Antony was never troubled, his soul being calm, and he never looked gloomy, his mind being joyous.

Lord, grant me a humble spirit to learn from everyone I meet, and a joyous spirit that shows itself outwardly.

June 23

PSALM 94:10–12   JEREMIAH 9:23   I CORINTHIANS 1:20–25

While Antony was living in the remote outer mountain, two Greek philosophers visited him, thinking they would be able to put him to the test. Antony was not a scholar and does not even appear to have spoken Greek; he probably only spoke the local language, Coptic. So the philosophers, dressed in the gowns that indicated their profession, would not have had a high opinion of his learning.

> Knowing what the men were from their appearance, he went out to them and said through an interpreter, 'Why did you go to so much trouble, you philosophers, to visit a foolish man?' When they responded that he was not foolish, but quite wise, he said to them, 'If you came to a foolish man, your toil is superfluous, but if you consider me wise, become as I am, for we must imitate what is good. If I had come to you I would have imitated you; but since you came to me, become as I am; for I am a Christian.' In amazement they withdrew, for they saw that even demons feared Antony.

Lord, help me to worship You with my mind, but save me from worshipping the achievements of my study; I want to be wise in Your wisdom.

June 24 *Bartholomew of Farne*

PSALM 49:10–13   MICAH 4:5   ROMANS 1:20–25

Others, similarly, came to Antony, thinking they would subject him to ridicule because he had not learned letters. To them Antony said, 'What do you say? Which is first – mind or letters? And which is the cause of which – the mind of the letters, or the letters of the mind?' When they replied that the mind is first, and an inventor of the letters, Antony spoke of how it is appropriate to admire created things, but not to idolize and worship them. Rather, we should give honour to the Creator.

We are created to worship God, yet often our worship gets diverted and we worship the reflection and not the One who is reflected. It seems that human beings are capable of worshipping just about anything: traditions, buildings, possessions, relationships, ideas – the list goes on. They may well be worthy of admiration, but the Lord alone is worthy of our praise.

Lord, thank You that there is so much in life to admire and enjoy. Help me to worship You, for You alone have made these things, and You alone give them to me.

June 25

PSALM 82:1, 3   PROVERBS 16:19–20   MATTHEW 7:1–2

When Antony healed the sick, he did not do so by his own commands, but by praying and calling on the name of Christ, so it was clear to all that it was not he who did this, but the Lord bringing His benevolence to effect through Antony and curing those who were afflicted. Only the prayer was Antony's. It was his discipline, not least in prayer and the contemplation of God in solitude, that made his prayers so powerful. If we would be powerful in prayer and spiritual gifts, then we need to spend much time alone with our Lord. On one occasion, when Antony refused to go and see some judges to give them advice, they had soldiers force him to come. They valued his help that much.

> Swayed then by necessity, and seeing these people lamenting, he went to the outer mountain … He aided the judges, advising them to value justice over everything else, and to fear God, and to realize that by the judgement with which they judged, they themselves would be judged. Nevertheless, he loved more than everything else his way of life in the mountain. He said, 'Just as fish perish when they lie exposed for a while on the dry land, so also the monks relax their discipline when they linger and pass time with you. Therefore, we must rush back to the mountain, like the fish to the sea – so that we might not, by remaining among you, forget the things within us.'

Lord, help me to make time for You in secret, deepening my walk and my understanding of Your ways.

June 26

PSALM 116:14–16   GENESIS 25:8   PHILIPPIANS 1:20–21

Even in his death Antony was exemplary. Coming to see the monks as usual, he told them that it would probably be the last time they would see him and that, at the age of 105, his life was coming to an end.

> When they heard him, they wept and embraced and kissed the old man. But he, like one sailing from a foreign city to his own, talked cheerfully and exhorted them not to lose heart in their labours nor to grow weary in the discipline, but to live as though dying daily. He told them, 'Be zealous in protecting the soul from foul thoughts, as I said before …

guard both the traditions of the fathers and especially the holy faith in our Lord Jesus Christ, which you have learned from the Scriptures and have often had recalled to you by me.'

A few months later he became ill and said to those with him, 'I am going the way of the fathers, as it is written, for I see myself being summoned by the Lord.' He encouraged them to preserve their enthusiasm, discipline and purity, telling them to 'strive always to be bound to each other as allies, first of all in the Lord, and then in the saints, so that after death *they may receive you into eternal habitations* as friends and companions' (Luke 16:9). Antony died, his face bright and cheerful.

Lord, thank You that You have made death a homecoming, a joyful passage into something infinitely better.

June 27

PSALM 102:18   PROVERBS 19:20   MATTHEW 5:14–16

Proof of his virtue and that his soul was loved by God is found in the fact that he is famous everywhere and is marvelled at by everyone and is dearly missed by people who never saw him. Neither from writing, nor from pagan wisdom, nor from some craft, was Antony acclaimed, but on account of religion alone. That this was something given by God no one would deny. For how is it that he was heard of, though concealed and sitting in a mountain, in Spain and Gaul, and in Rome and Africa, unless it was the God who everywhere makes His trusted ones known who also promised this to Antony in the beginning? For even though they themselves act in secret, and may want to be forgotten, nevertheless the Lord shows them like lamps to everyone, so that those who hear may know that the commandments have power for amendment of life, and may gain zeal for the way of virtue.

Therefore, read these things now to the other brothers so that they may learn what the life of the monks ought to be, and so they may believe that our Lord and Saviour Jesus Christ glorifies those who glorify Him, and not only leads those who serve Him to the end into the kingdom of heaven, but even here, though they conceal themselves and seek to retire, He makes them known and celebrated everywhere, both because of their own virtue and because of their assistance to others.

Lord, may I be a blessing to You and a blessing to Your people; but never for my glory, always for Yours.

June 28 *Irenaeus*

PSALM 123:2   DEUTERONOMY 29:29   HEBREWS 11:6; 12:2

Someone asked Abba Antony, 'What must one do in order to please God?' The old man replied, 'Pay attention to what I tell you:

whoever you may be, always have God before
your eyes;
whatever you do, do it according to the testimony
of the holy Scriptures;
in whatever place you live, do not easily leave it.
Keep these three precepts and you will be saved.'

Lord, help me so to order my life that it may be pleasing to You.

June 29

PSALM 51:10–13   JOB 33:26–28   MATTHEW 6:12–15

It happened one day that one of the brethren in the monastery of Abba Elias was tempted. Cast out of the monastery, he went over the mountain to Abba Antony. The brother lived near him for a while and then Antony sent him back to the monastery from which he had been expelled. When the brothers saw him they cast him out yet again, and he went back to Abba Antony saying, 'Father, they will not receive me.'

Then the old man sent them a message saying, 'A boat was shipwrecked at sea and lost its cargo; with great difficulty it reached the shore; but you want to throw into the sea that which has found a safe harbour on the shore.' When the brothers understood that it was Abba Antony who had sent them this monk, they received him at once.

Lord, please help me to forgive and bear with my forgiven brothers and sisters, for I too sin and stand in constant need of Your mercy and help.

June 30

PSALM 91:1–2   ISAIAH 57:2   HEBREWS 4:9–13

A hunter in the desert saw Abba Antony enjoying himself with the brothers and he was shocked. Wanting to show him that it was necessary sometimes to meet the needs of the brothers, the old man said to him, 'Put an arrow in your bow and shoot it.' So he did. The old man then said, 'Shoot another,' and he did so. Then the old man said to him, 'Shoot yet again,' and the hunter replied, 'If I bend my bow so much I will break it.' Then the old man said to him, 'It is the same with the work of God. If we stretch our brothers beyond measure they will soon break. Sometimes it is necessary to come down to meet their needs.' When he heard these words the hunter was pierced by compunction and, greatly edified by the old man, he went away. As for those brothers, they went home strengthened.

Lord, help me to know when to relax a little and rest in You, for You have commanded rest!

July

LITTLE BROTHER OF JESUS

The background information for this month's readings is drawn from *The Sands of Tamanrasset*, a life of Charles de Foucauld by Marion Mill Preminger. Brother Charles of Jesus, who lived and died in poverty among the tribespeople of the Sahara, was from a rich French family and had been a playboy, a soldier and an explorer at earlier stages in his life. Dramatically converted to Christ, he became a monk, but found even the Trappist order not demanding enough, and lived out his vocation as a hermit and finally also as a priest. The Communities of Little Brothers and Sisters of Jesus sprang up only after his death. He was betrayed by his own servant and murdered by bandits from a fanatical Muslim sect. The readings are supplemented by quotes from Charles de Foucauld's writings in *Meditations of a Hermit* and *Letters from the Desert*. We acknowledge that the life of Charles de Foucauld following his conversion was one of great austerity and some of his practices were most certainly extreme. We do not wish to imply that these be imitated by all. What we can all seek to emulate, however, is his example of single-hearted devotion to God.

July 1

PSALM 102:24   ISAIAH 53:7–9   ACTS 5:41

At the end of the eighteenth century the Archbishop of Arles and his cousin Armand de Foucauld were slaughtered in the bloody revolution in France because they were believers. Armand was just 41 years old. His last wish was that he would not be the last in his family to die for the glory of his Lord. They did not hear the swish of the sabre, nor the gleam of late sunlight on the pikes. They were on their knees praying when they fell – the 119th and 120th martyrs to die that Sunday afternoon. It would be more than a century before Armand's last wish could be fulfilled.

Charles Eugène de Foucauld, great-grand-nephew of the martyred Armand, was born in Strasbourg on September 15 1858. He gave no sign in his early years of great piety or dedication to the cause of the Lord. In fact, he was considered a rather nasty little boy, fat, headstrong, and stubbornly self-centred.

His father, a civil servant, was a nervous, high-strung man, frequently in ill health. Charles remembered him only vaguely because he was so often away from home. Whatever piety Charles absorbed in his childhood he got from his mother, who died in 1864 at the age of 34. Her husband died – by his own hand, according to some – a few months after the death of his wife, bequeathing to his young son Charles the title of Viscount.

The boy and his sister, Marie, were adopted by their maternal grandfather. The indulgent old gentleman spoiled his charges, particularly Charles, whose tantrums he considered a sign of character.

July 2

PSALM 24:1   PROVERBS 22:2   I TIMOTHY 5:17–19

While he was in the lovely Loire valley for a year's specialized training at the Cavalry School, Second Lieutenant Charles devoted himself to changing his inheritance into pleasure. The room that he and his aristocratic room-mate occupied was always well stocked with the finest wines in France. When he entertained in town, he took his guests to the best restaurant in Saumur.

Hardly a week passed without the wealthy second lieutenant being confined to his luxurious quarters for some breach of discipline – shoes not shined, bed improperly made, failure to observe lights out, requesting sick leave when in perfect health...

> Teach me to prolong these hours in which I watch alone at Your feet. Everything sleeps, no one knows of my happiness nor shares it. I rejoice through the solitude of the night in Your presence, O my God.

July 3 Thomas

PSALM 139:15–16   PROVERBS 15:3   I TIMOTHY 5:24–25

There is no record for which military sin the Viscount was aton-
ing one afternoon when he was stretched out on his Louis XV
divan, sipping champagne and eating with a golden spoon. He
had been confined to his quarters by the Commandant, and he
was going to miss the gala ball at Tours that evening.

He had, however, arranged for the most fashionable barber in
Saumur to shave him. An hour later the sentry at the exit gate of
the Cavalry School waved through a plump, bearded man in civil-
ian clothes, carrying what was obviously a barber's home-service
kit. At the same moment, the master barber was reclining on the
Viscount's Louis XV sofa, rinsing his mouth with vintage champagne. Charles was discovered at the ball with his beautiful
blonde girlfriend Mimi. She could not resist pulling his beard.
Her plump companion's chin whiskers came off in her hand,
dropped from her fingers and splashed into the champagne.
Charles was confined to quarters for a further three weeks.

> Quite apart from my own will, events occurred which
> forced me to detach myself from material things that had
> such charm for me and which would have held back my
> soul and kept me tied to the world. These ties You broke
> violently like so many others. How good You are, my God,
> to have broken up and destroyed all around me those things
> that might have kept me from belonging to You alone. You
> gave me a profound sense of the vanity and falseness of the
> world, the vast gulf that lies between the perfect life of the
> Gospel, and that which one leads in the world. You gave me
> a tender and a growing love for You, my Lord Jesus, a love
> of prayer, of faith in Your words, a deep sense of the duty of
> almsgiving and a great desire to imitate You.

July 4

PSALM 53:2   ECCLESIASTES 5:19–20   JAMES 1:16–17

Charles was assigned to the Fourth Hussars, garrisoned in Lorraine. The colourful uniform of an officer seemed to bring out the last extravagant ounce of all that was rebellious and licentious in character of the young Viscount.

All the junior officers were invited to partake of the wines and choice viands, the music and the feminine laughter that were the mark of a riotous Foucauld party – with the result that often the Viscount was asked to seek new lodgings. He delighted in giving one of his parties on evenings when the commander of the Fourth Hussars was entertaining the senior officers. He would hire every taxi in town so that the Colonel's guests were without transportation. On one such occasion, when he was confined to quarters and forbidden to receive visitors, he again hired the taxis and had them line up outside his quarters. He turned on all his lights and played the piano loudly, occasionally shrieking with laughter. When the officer of the day arrived with instructions from the Colonel to arrest all those who were helping the profligate to while away the boring hours of his punishment, they found only Charles, sitting alone at the piano, wide-eyed with innocent surprise.

His girlfriend Mimi was a dancer of small talent but great physical appeal. A girl of humble origin, she grew sincerely fond of Charles, was tenderly responsive to all his moods and always tried to please him. In return she had the best Paris couturiers at her service in a suite at the best hotel, and a yellow-wheeled cart in which she could follow the Fourth Hussars on parade. Mimi was strictly barred from meeting Charles' family, however.

> What mercy You have shown me. Mercy in the past, in the present, at every minute of my life, before my birth and before all time. I am drowned, flooded in these mercies, they envelop and protect me on all sides.

I sinned, but neither approved of, nor loved sin. You made me feel in it such emptiness and sadness as I have never felt at any other time. It came upon me when I found myself alone in my room at night, it made me dumb and miserable in the midst of what others call festivities. I was the moving spirit in these, but in the midst of them I felt dumb, disgusted, infinitely bored.

At no other time have I felt such sadness, depression and unrest. So, my God, it was a gift from You. I was very far from realizing it.

July 5

PSALM 93:1–2   PROVERBS 12:1; 15:32   HEBREWS 12:5–11

The Commandant wanted to keep the Viscount in the army. He thought that Charles would make a good soldier because he had character and the stubborn courage of his principles, even if these were often distorted. He said, 'When he learns discipline, he will be a first-class officer. Strong. His strength burns in his eyes.'

When the Fourth Hussars left for Africa, Mimi crossed the Mediterranean in style. The Viscount had engaged a deluxe cabin for her on a ship sailing from Marseilles several days ahead of the transport bearing the regiment. Her name appeared on the passenger list as Madame la Vicomtesse de Foucauld. She carried off the role of Viscountess with great charm, but was shrewd enough to get out of town before the arrival of the regiment and the wives of the senior officers. She went on ahead to prepare quarters for Monsieur le Vicomte de Foucauld. The uproar that followed this breach of protocol almost ended Charles' military career, and he was sent home from Africa.

Our Lord came to find that which was lost. He leaves the sheep that are safe in the fold and sets out to look for the one that has wandered away. Let us do like Him, and since our prayers are a force and since they are certain to obtain what they ask, we should fly to the rescue of sinners.

Let us pray every day with all our heart for the salvation
and sanctification of all those wandering souls that were so
much beloved by our Lord, that they may not perish, but be
happy. Let us pray every day for them, at great length and
with all our hearts, so that the heart of Jesus may be con-
soled by their conversion and rejoiced by their salvation.

July 6

PSALM 36:5–9   JEREMIAH 15:16   I JOHN 2:17

Charles decided that he was a soldier and the descendant of soldiers; that the family motto *Jamais arrière* meant more than stubborn resistance to a colonel's order to send his mistress back to
France. He must at all costs return to Africa. Mimi found him
impervious to her attentions for the first time, and realized that
a radical change was going on within him. She silently withdrew,
leaving him still sitting in his chair, apparently unaware of
her presence. She was not surprised, therefore, when Charles
announced that night that they were leaving immediately for
Paris. In Paris he went at once to the War Ministry to ask for a
return to active duty.

On June 3 1881 he was restored to his rank as second lieutenant of cavalry and ordered to rejoin his old regiment in Africa.
Bronzed and lean from active service, the others had already shed
blood in combat. The married officers were still resentful of the
domestic trouble Charles had caused them by flaunting his mistress, and greeted him coldly. The one old friend of cadet days
who did welcome him was Lieutenant Henri Laperrine, now
wildly in love with Africa.

For ten years I did not believe in God. How good You were.
I escaped marvellously from riding accidents, duels were
averted, dangerous expeditions were carried through without disaster, You brought me miraculously through perilous

journeys, You gave me health in poisonous climates and in great fatigues. O my God, Your hand was leading me and I felt it so little. How good You are. How You have kept and guarded me. You sheltered me under Your wings when I did not even believe in Your existence.

July 7 *Boisil*

PSALM 102:25   ISAIAH 40:21–26   REVELATION 4:11

Charles was refused a dangerous expedition and he resigned from the army. He was 23 years old. He asked permission to withdraw to his home in Paris, but did not return there, eventually going on expeditions in north Africa that culminated in him travelling in disguise for safety.

During his months disguised as a rabbi, he travelled nearly 2,000 miles on foot and on mule-back, some 1,400 miles further than previous explorers, whose data he corrected. He logged the latitude and longitude of 40 localities and corrected the longitude of five others. He fixed the altitude above sea level of 3,000 points, where only a few dozen had been recorded previously. He described in lucid and sometimes poetic terms the geography of a virtually unknown sultanate, and outlined the social and racial structure of various tribes and their political relationship with, or independence of, the Sultan.

He made a sociological and statistical study of the Jews in Morocco and mapped all the roads he travelled by working out the travel time by foot and by mule for each stage. He did the same for the principal rivers and their tributaries and made more than 100 sketches. He also made a census of the number of horses and firearms possessed by the various tribes. When he had finished, he was not yet 26 years old.

If we ask You for dangerous playthings You refuse them in goodness for us, and You console us by giving us other things for our good. If we ask You to put us where it would be dangerous for us to be You do not give us what is not for our good, but You give us something really for our welfare, something that we would ask for ourselves if our eyes were open. You take us by the hand and lead us, not there where we would wish to go, but there where it is best for us to be.

July 8

PSALM 102:9   PROVERBS 20:6   PHILIPPIANS 2:3–4

Charles called on a retired army officer in Algiers, a geographer of note called Major Titre, to discuss some maps and, as it happened, met the major's daughter. It was apparently love at first sight, but he also saw in her the answer to his hopes and the materialization of his dreams. He was, she wrote many years later, the great love – the only love – of her life. To Charles, she was not only the incarnation of the love he had been vainly seeking all his life, but she represented stability.

She would make an excellent wife, he decided. She came of a bourgeois family from Lyons, was born a Protestant but had become a pious Catholic. The agnostic Foucauld told her he would not interfere in her practice of whatever religion she wished. She told him she was sure that in time he would return to the Church. He asked the geographer for his daughter's hand in marriage.

He went home for a family Christmas, his first in years, and stayed for his sister's wedding. Until then, Charles had given his family in France no inkling of his impending marriage. He expected them to be delighted with his news that he also was to settle down at last, and was surprised that they were not at all pleased. His aunt, aghast, said that a Foucauld must not be a traitor to his class and dilute his bloodline by marrying a commoner.

His cousin Marie realized that he loved this girl very much, but she told him that he must give her up because he would make her very unhappy. Charles was totally absorbed in researching a book he was writing about the oases of the Sahara and the salt marshes of Tunisia. How could he marry when at any moment he could be rushing off to the Congo or Madagascar? Marie also told him he should never marry – he should become a monk.

Charles took her words to heart. He did not see Mademoiselle Titre on his return, but explained to her father that, as he was planning another journey of African exploration, he would like, with infinite regrets, to withdraw his offer of marriage. He hoped the geographer and explorer would understand that this would be the best for all concerned.

July 9

PSALM 102:1   JEREMIAH 29:12–14A   ACTS 17:23–28A

By day Charles worked at the last draft of his book on Morocco. By night he led an active social life which centred around the town house of his Aunt Inès. Her Sunday 'at homes' were attended by the cream of Parisian society and the world of politics, arts and letters.

One regular attendee at dinners or on Sundays intrigued Charles: the Reverend Father Huvelin. Abbé Huvelin was a man of reason and a man whose sermons were not addressed to old ladies, but attracted intellectuals to St Augustin's Church when he was preaching. When Charles first met him, he was still in his forties. His piercing eyes might have seen all the world's sadness and tragedy.

Charles did not approach the Abbé directly for some time. First of all, he was busy correcting his Moroccan book. Second, he was still dependent on his cousin Marie in matters of the spirit. In their long and frequent talks, he told her that she was lucky to believe because, as much as he sought the light, he could not find it. Her advice was, 'Pray.'

Sometimes on his way home from his aunt's brilliant soirées, still sporting white tie and tails, he would drop in at a church and would follow the counsel of his beloved cousin. It was always the same prayer: 'If Thou art my God, make Thyself known to me, O Lord!'

There was no answer.

July 10

PSALM 102:19–20   PROVERBS 9:10; 28:13   I JOHN 1:8–9; 4:9–10

One morning in late October 1886 Charles arose very early, unable to sleep. His steps seemed to be directed to the Place Saint Augustin. He strode into the church and went directly to the confessional he knew to be occupied by the Abbé Huvelin. He said, 'I have no faith. I come to ask you to teach me.' The priest ordered him to kneel. 'Confess your sins to God,' he said, 'then you will believe.' Charles protested that this was not what he had come for. 'On your knees!' said the Abbé. 'Confess!'

Viscount Charles de Foucauld, the cadet who made a shambles of discipline, the subaltern who defied the French army because of a blue-eyed blonde, the man who braved death in hostile Morocco, knelt obediently and humbly recited the guilty details of his lurid past. At last the Abbé sent him to Communion. Charles seemed a little dazed as he rose to his feet, but he walked towards the altar rail with a light, buoyant step.

> When You made me enter Abbé Huvelin's confessional one day at the end of October (between the 27th and 30th I think it was), You gave me the best of all, my God. If there is joy in heaven for one sinner that repents there must have been joy the day that I went into the confessional. Since that day my life has been one long series of blessings. You put me under the wings of that saint and there I stayed. You have borne me along by his hands and I have received one grace after another. I asked him for instruction in religion, and he made me kneel down and make my confession and

sent me straight away to Communion. I cannot help weeping when I think of it, and would not if I could, for it is right that I should still weep tears of gratitude at the remembrance of such mercies. How good You have been.

Charles' conversion, like so many other recorded experiences, was instantaneous, like a great light suddenly bursting upon him after so many years of wandering in the dark. His festering doubt vanished as though it had never existed. He had never experienced any feeling of guilt or sin, but now the great weight of brooding incompleteness, the heavy sense of imperfection, was abruptly lifted. He truly felt himself a new man. For a while there was no external sign of the change, except that he now attended Mass regularly and his friends noted that he seemed to smile more frequently.

July 11

PSALM 102:12   JEREMIAH 31:33–34   PHILIPPIANS 3:7–9

At the age of 32, Charles entered a Trappist community. Before he left Paris he knelt beside his beloved cousin Marie at the altar rail. Together they listened while Abbé Huvelin celebrated Mass. This would be their last day together. They roamed the grey streets of Paris like the lovers they had never been nor would ever be. They said little, for there was no need for words. Their hearts were full of the great and pure love Marie had changed into a complete, burning passion for God. The man she had rescued from himself, she was giving to the Lord. The joy of the sacrifice must outweigh the sorrow of parting.

After they said goodbye, Charles wept. He later wrote:

This sacrifice has cost me all my tears. Since that time, since that day, I no longer weep. I seem to have no more tears to shed, except sometimes when I remember. The wound of 15th January is always the same. The sacrifice of that day remains the sacrifice of every hour.

The next day he wrote to Marie:

> How can I thank you for the sweetness of these last days, of these last hours, of yesterday? ... May we be reunited some day at the feet of our Lord, communing with Him as we did yesterday morning, receiving His blessing as I received yours last evening. Sweet benediction!

Twenty-seven years later, when he wrote to her just before his death, it would be the 734th such letter he would send to her. In it he said:

> It seems we do not love enough. But the good Lord, who knows from what mud He has fashioned us, has told us that none who come to Him shall ever be rejected.

July 12

PSALM 102:5, 27   PROVERBS 22:4   PHILIPPIANS 2:5–8; 3:10–11

Charles had chosen to be a Trappist monk because he found the rule of the order to be the strictest and most trying, and he had chosen Our Lady of the Snows because he considered it the poorest monastery he had visited. He was resolved to lead a life of poverty, humility, abnegation and self-effacement, as close to the suffering of Jesus Christ as he could manage. 'I cannot bear living a life of ease and honours,' he wrote, 'when our Lord's was the ultimate of suffering and scorn. I cannot travel through life in first class when He whom I love travelled in the lowest...'

He asked to be transferred to a Trappist monastery in Syria which he had been told was even more impoverished, where life was even more primitive, and which would entail the self-punishment of exile from the France he loved. Six months after he became a Trappist, his request was granted.

During his first years in Syria, there were three successive epidemics of cholera which not only swept the villages but invaded the monasteries as well. He soothed fevered limbs, washed pain-racked bodies, prayed for tormented souls and comforted the dying. In the midst of death, he thought for the first time of consecrating not only his life to God, but his death as well. As he wrote to his cousin Marie, the good Lord had evidently found him not yet ready for death.

After three years in Syria, Charles was practically certain that he would never take his final vows as a Trappist. The order which he had chosen because of its harsh rule, its stark poverty and rigorous piety was becoming too soft for him.

His dissatisfaction was increased when he was sent to comfort the family of a Christian Syrian peasant who was dying of cholera a few miles from the monastery. When he saw the misery, the filth and the bare subsistence that marked the lives of these simple people, he burst into tears. It was with a deep sense of shame that he left the wretched hut of the cholera victim to re-enter what seemed to him the comparative luxury of his austere Trappist cloisters.

July 13

PSALM 84:1–4   SONG OF SONGS 2:3–7; 6:3A   LUKE 7:36–50

Charles began to formulate plans for what was to become a life-long obsession: a congregation more austere than the Trappists, closer to the life of Christ:

> No current order of the Church provides the possibility of leading the life which He Himself led in this world; might I not be able to recruit a few souls to form the nucleus of a small congregation of this kind?

The rules would be simple but hard. Absolute poverty. Manual labour sufficient to maintain the brothers on a subsistence level, but enough to give generously to the poor. Prayers without end. And there was to be no hierarchy – everyone was to be a Little Brother or Little Sister of Jesus.

> Pray a lot: when we love we want to talk endlessly to the one-and-only we love, or at least to look at Him endlessly. This is what prayer is, familiar converse with our Beloved: we look at Him, we tell Him we love Him, we rejoice at being at His feet, we tell Him that this is where we want to live and die.

July 14

PSALM 62:5–8   PROVERBS 8:12, 17–21   MATTHEW 13:44–46

In January 1897, Abbé Huvelin repeated advice he had given to Charles before, to return to the Holy Land and live alone. He wrote: 'Live in the shadow of a monastery but not in it, using only its spiritual resources, and living in poverty at its door. Do not dream of grouping a company of souls around you, and especially do not dream of giving them a rule.' Early in February, no longer bound by Trappist vows, de Foucauld took his own personal vows of perpetual chastity and poverty.

Brother Charles of Jesus, as he now called himself, landed at Jaffa on February 24 1897. He made his way to Nazareth on foot, begging his food as he passed through Ramleh, Bethlehem and Jerusalem, sleeping in the fields. It took him 10 days to reach the shores of the Sea of Galilee, but it was like coming home.

At Nazareth, Mother Marie de Saint Michel of the Poor Clares at once employed the shabby pilgrim whom she found praying prostrate on the floor of her chapel. In fact, she knew the identity of her new handyman. The Franciscan hostel where Charles had stayed had recognized the traveller from his visit nine years before. They had advised Mother Marie that the man who would apply for a job as gardener was actually Viscount Charles de Foucauld. She kept his secret.

July 15

PSALM 89:15–17A   I CHRONICLES 28:9–10   MATTHEW 20:5–13

Brother Charles of Jesus wrote from Nazareth:

> Since my arrival in the Holy Land I have become a servant or rather a labourer, a day labourer, with the Poor Clares of Nazareth; I have the independence of a labourer, working in my own time and accepting only the work I want, like Mary's workman-son. I organize my time so as to earn my bread honestly, and the rest of the time I spend in front of the blessed Sacrament...
>
> During those thirty years You were, as a son, always tender, considerate, sympathetic, kind.
>
> This was Your life at Nazareth, and it is my infinite happiness and incomparable grace to live in this beloved Nazareth. Yours was the life of a model son with Your humble working parents. It made up half of Your life, that half that was of the earth has spread a heavenly perfume through heaven...
>
> I must believe no work beneath me, since Jesus was a carpenter for thirty years, and Joseph all his life. With this example I should, on the contrary, look upon any occupation or work as a great privilege. I must welcome with love and readiness any occasion for humility, any humiliation that emulates the humility of Jesus. Since, if my sins were known to others, nothing would seem to them bad enough for me, let me avoid all lofty occupations and all high positions because Jesus was lowly and despised. I must accept no promotion whatever it may be, unless only obedience

imposes it on me and if I see that it is a duty and the will of God...

I live in a wooden shack outside the cloister. This is exactly the life I have been seeking...

I live an enclosed life and keep the silence; it is God Himself who had led me as if by the hand into this haven which He seems to have prepared for me. I cannot praise Him enough for what I have found here: recollection and retreat, and the poverty and abjection of a labourer I have wanted for so long. So now you know all about my very simple life which is becoming more and more hidden.

The wooden shack was actually a small tool shed. He had refused to sleep in the gardener's room within the compound, because he found it much too elegant. He even discarded the straw pallet and blanket that he had at first taken into the shed, and thereafter slept on a bench with a stone for a pillow.

July 16

PSALM 143:10   JEREMIAH 7:23   I THESSALONIANS 5:16–18

My God, here am I at Your feet in my cell, all around is in silence, all sleeps. I am perhaps the only soul in Nazareth, at this moment at Your feet.

Thank You, thank You. I am grateful. I adore You from the depths of my soul.

Ought I to cling to staying at Nazareth? No, not more than to anything else. I should cling to nothing but the will of God. I should feel that it is a great grace to live at Nazareth, be happy in it and be grateful, but I should not attach myself to it.

As soon as it is no longer the will of God that I should stay here, I should leave instantly without hesitation, or backward look, and go wherever His will calls me.

July 17

PSALM 102:13–14   ISAIAH 30:15–18   MATTHEW 6:5–13

At a convent near Jerusalem, Mother Elizabeth welcomed Charles and his attempt to form his Little Brothers of Jesus. She gave permission for a little nucleus of such a colony to be housed close to her convent. Brother Charles settled down for a while in the shack next to the watchman's cottage outside the convent walls. He wrote to his family:

> My life here is the same as at Nazareth, except that I am even more alone, which is still better. The convent is two kilometres from Jerusalem on the road to Bethany, on an admirable site beside the Vale of Kedron across from the Mount of Olives. All Jerusalem is spread beneath its windows, Gethsemane, the whole Mount of Olives, Bethany, the mountains of Moab and Idumea which rise like a dark wall beyond the Jordan...

He was kept busy with odd jobs, and particularly with the painting and drawing talents that he had almost forgotten after the last sketches for his work on Morocco. He painted religious subjects and made sketches for a new monastery. He received his own key to the chapel so that he might on occasion spend all night in prayer.

July 18

PSALM 102:15–17   I SAMUEL 16:7   I CORINTHIANS 1:26–31

Mother Elizabeth made a suggestion, one that would not only take him back to the region that he preferred, but might well lay the cornerstone for his dream project, a home for his Little Brothers. How would he like to take title to the Mount of the

Beatitudes on the shore of the Sea of Galilee? What a perfect spot for a holy hermitage, an isolated place where the nucleus of the Little Brothers of Jesus might grow, and yet a shrine which might become a goal of really hardy and saintly pilgrims. Brother Charles was intoxicated by the idea.

The Franciscans, in turn, put him in touch with their Jerusalem business agent, who said he could help secure title to the Mount of the Beatitudes site for 13,000 francs. Charles' enthusiasm knew no bounds. He wrote to his brother-in-law, asking him to send him the 13,000 francs at once.

Just at this time, Mother Marie at Nazareth wrote to Charles saying that there was trouble over the title to the land upon which his tool-shed sanctuary stood. She asked if he would come and help straighten things out. He went at once. The land dispute was ultimately settled in favour of the Poor Clares, largely because Brother Charles re-established residence in the tool shed.

His status as a prospective landowner was making less progress, however. Inexplicable delays, curious complications and requests for new documents were forever coming up. He suspected that the Turkish government was behind the delay, and he was right. Turkish censors had been reading all his incoming and outgoing mail, and they were puzzled. Here was a penniless pilgrim, a ragamuffin who lived in a shanty outside the Clarist convent, yet who wrote and received letters to and from viscounts, marquises, generals and archbishops. Furthermore, Turkish intelligence reported that Brother Charles of Jesus was actually none other than Viscount Charles de Foucauld, a former officer of the Fourth Hussars and Fourth Chasseurs d'Afrique, who had undertaken a hazardous mission into Morocco, obviously for the purpose of mapping the interior for the French Army.

Here was a supposedly penniless religious ascetic who, practically overnight, was able to put down 13,000 francs on an otherwise worthless piece of real estate – worthless except that it was a mountain top. It would be an ideal observation post. He must be subject to the most careful scrutiny.

July 19

PSALM 102:10   ISAIAH 55:8–9   JOHN 6:38

> The human mind may devise many plans,
> but it is the purpose of the Lord that will be established.
>
> *Proverbs 19:21*

In June 1900 Brother Charles walked to Jerusalem to see the Patriarch. First of all, he needed the Patriarch's permission to be ordained in his diocese. Second, he needed the Patriarch's authority to establish his hermitage atop the Mount of the Beatitudes. And finally, he wanted the Patriarch's approval of his rule for the congregation of the Little Brothers of Jesus which he expected to grow on the sacred mountain top.

The Patriarch listened impatiently while Brother Charles expounded his case, then said, 'We will consider the matter. Please withdraw now.' As Charles wrote later, 'I saw the Patriarch and told him what I had to say. So although he dismissed me in a rather cavalier manner, I am quite content. I could not be at greater peace or more happy.'

The Patriarch kept his promise to consider the matter and summoned him to another interview for further discussion of his plans, but it was too late. Charles had accepted the Patriarch's initial dismissal as a token of the Divine Will. God apparently did not approve of his plans to become a priest and remain in the Holy Land as chaplain of a shrine on the Mount of the Beatitudes. There was no use, therefore, in returning to discuss the matter further with His Excellency. He had made up his mind to become a priest; there was no Divine indication of disapproval of this decision. Therefore, if he could not become a priest in Jerusalem, he would return to France.

He sought to recover the 13,000 francs he had paid for the Mount of the Beatitudes, so that he could return the money to his brother-in-law. In this, too, he met with rejection. Either because of the Turkish government or some sharp real-estate operators, Brother Charles owned nothing but a receipt for 13,000 francs. The man whose signature was on his receipt had fled Jerusalem. Title to the Mount of Beatitudes had been sold to somebody else.

Brother Charles was no longer to be deterred from his new purpose, however: Paris and priesthood. Paris – for the first time in 10 years!

July 20

PSALM 146:5–10   DEUTERONOMY 7:7–9   EPHESIANS 3:7–9

After training for the priesthood, Charles returned to Africa and became a chaplain to a small French garrison on the edge of the Sahara desert. On December 1 1901 he celebrated his first Mass in his new chapel. It was packed with officers and men from the garrison, some curious, many devout, many hungry for the spiritual life they had been missing for so long. One soldier wrote: 'He recited the "Lord, I am not worthy" with such feeling that we all wanted to cry with him.'

Charles was both surprised and pleased to find so many soldiers coming to his primitive chapel for Mass, for confession and for his informal evenings to listen to his exposition of the gospel. In every case, he sent the soldier a letter, asking him to come back whenever he felt like it and could get away from the garrison. These letters he signed 'Brother Charles of Jesus', because he felt that if the men considered him a real chaplain, probably with officer rank, they would feel shy. For this he was rewarded by a continuous stream of these French soldiers.

His mud chapel measured about 45 feet in length, 13 feet in width and 13 feet in height. While his establishment was expanding, Charles slept at the foot of the altar, 'curled up like a dog at the feet of his master'. Little by little he added outbuildings, including narrow cells, in one of which he would sleep for the few hours he allowed himself to rest. When an officer of the garrison asked how he could possibly sleep since there was no room to stretch out full length and relax, Charles replied: 'Did Jesus have room to relax on the cross?'

The cells of the Little Brothers – who never came – were just as narrow. The room for passing travellers was bigger. Charles was now feeding 75 indigents a day, aside from his freed slaves. He needed help: manpower rather than money – or womenpower if he could get it, although he hesitated to ask for nuns to be sent to this primitive oasis. He wrote:

> I am still alone. I need companions, but apparently I am not sufficiently faithful that Jesus could give me even one. I do my best to follow the little rule that you know so well...

The 'little rule' which everyone knew 'so well' was still the willingness to starve to death, to shed blood gladly on African soil, to obey Brother Charles blindly, despite his unworthiness. There were no takers.

> Here there is much to be done, for natives and officers and men: there are 200 Christian soldiers, very many natives, most of them poor, many poor travelling Arabs; alms, hospitality, charity, kindness, can do a great deal of good among the Muslims and dispose them to know Jesus. A lot of good can be done for the soldiers too: I hope some of them will go to Communion at midnight Mass, I hope to be able to draw them to me so as to draw them to Jesus.

July 21

PSALM 102:3–4   JOSHUA 1:7–8   I CORINTHIANS 10:12–13

In the following extract from Charles de Foucauld's desert journal, he is being addressed by Jesus:

I let the devil tempt Me in the desert for you, for love of you and for your instruction; that you might know in the first place that there is greater temptation in the desert than elsewhere and that those who, for love of Me, choose the solitary life, must be neither surprised nor discouraged by the multiplicity of its temptations. Further you should understand that temptation is not sin, since I Myself was tempted by monstrous things.

Therefore you should neither be distressed nor discouraged when you are tempted; and finally that you may see how to resist temptation. It must be resisted at once, as soon as it appears, from the first instant. A good way to fight temptations is to confront them with words of Holy Scripture which draw divine strength from their source.

July 22

PSALM 102:6, 7, 28   JEREMIAH 15:15–18   JOHN 16:32

Don't you think you would obtain a little glory for Jesus if you sent me someone, for as soon as I have just one zealous companion I shall be able to have exposition of the blessed Sacrament for quite a few hours *every day*.

My guests – the poor, my slaves, my visitors – never leave me alone for a moment; I am on my own for all the duties of the monastery. Ever since the little guest house was completed there have been guests for supper, bed and breakfast every day, not counting a cripple who is here all the time; I usually have between 60 and 100 visitors a day. So you see how much I need a companion. If he can be satisfied with little more than bread and water he will not die of hunger.

If you find a soul capable of being a good religious, prepared to follow me, ready to face martyrdom, to die of hunger and obey faithfully, send him to me, if you think that is Jesus' will.

The one man who tried to join him as a Little Brother left after two or three months on doctor's advice. Brother Michel describes his time there:

> The seven or eight cells designed for future monks were so low that the average man could easily touch the ceiling with his hand, so narrow that he could touch opposite walls with outstretched arms. No bed, no chairs, no table, no prie-dieu to kneel upon. A man had to sleep in his clothes stretched out on a palm-leaf mat on the ground. The sacristy was fairly large and served the Father as library, store room, bedroom, and study ... During the long offices and pious practices all day and night, we had to stand or kneel or squat on mats.
>
> We spent Christmas 1906 at the hermitage. At midnight Mass a hundred officers, NCOs and soldiers filled both the chapel and the sacristy.

July 23 *John Cassian*

PSALM 102:18   ISAIAH 42:5–7   MATTHEW 5:13–16

> To him who seeks the kingdom of God all the rest shall be added...

Charles had no followers in his lifetime, but his seed of hope, prayer and example was faithfully planted, and in its time has yielded rich growth.

The Little Brothers of Jesus were founded in 1932 in Algeria. Fraternities had been established in 25 different countries by 1977. These are small groups living according to the principles of poverty, hospitality and adoration of the blessed Sacrament – whether in the desert proper or in the wilderness of urban centres.

The Little Sisters of Jesus were founded in the Sahara in 1939 and (in 1977) numbered over 1,100 sisters in 200 fraternities of 50 different nationalities.

The Jesus/Caritas fraternity, started in 1954, is a wide-ranging group of men and women who do not necessarily become religious, priests or nuns. They devote themselves to Brother Charles' principles of living in a context of poverty, chastity and obedience, rather than preaching the presence of Christ in the world: 'Your vocation is to shout the gospel from the rooftops, not in words, but with your life.'

July 24

PSALM 102:22   ISAIAH 45:22–24A   REVELATION 15:2B–4

Brother Charles was always the charmer, toothless and hairless though he might be, to the female aristocracy near his chapel in the Hoggar Mountains the Sahara. They loved him. What a pity that such a good man was not a Muslim! One woman whose five children he had saved from starvation during the famine of 1907 told him that she prayed to Allah every night that Brother Charles would see the light and accept Islam.

Charles, on the other hand, encouraged the ladies to practise their own religion. He taught them to make rosaries – without a cross – from olive seeds and date pits. They were long ones, because each pit called for a prayer. As they told their beads, the ladies were supposed to say, 'I love Thee, O God,' for every small seed and, 'I love Thee with all my heart, O God,' for the big ones. There was only one God, wasn't there?

July 25

PSALM 102:11–23   ISAIAH 12:1–6   ROMANS 1:15–16

The Prefect in the Hoggar region sent an appeal to Rome on behalf of Brother Charles:

For six years this very saintly priest has unceasingly led a most admirable and heroic life in the apostolic prefecture of Ghardaïa. He is currently alone among the savage tribes whom he has succeeded in pacifying and to whom he has offered the fine example of his life of extreme poverty, inexhaustible charity, and continuous prayer. For many years to come he will doubtless be the only priest able to penetrate into the heart of this country. Therefore the Prefect Apostolic of Ghardaïa very humbly begs Your Holiness, in consideration of the outstanding virtues of this servant of God and of the very great good that he has accomplished, to deign to grant him the great favour...

The favour was Vatican approval for Brother Charles to celebrate Mass without a server. The Papal dispensation reached him on 31 January 1908. The relief to him was such that it seemed to lead to a complete physical collapse, and he became weak and ill.

> I would shout the gospel all my life.
> Convert my heart
> and let me glorify You to the utmost till my last breath
> and through all eternity.

July 26

PSALM 32:7–10   ISAIAH 30:19–21   MATTHEW 28:20B

Charles decided to take one of his parishioners to France to show him how a decent French family lived, and how good European Christians worshipped God and followed the teachings of Jesus Christ. By mid-1912 he had settled on his candidate – Ouksem, the young tribal chieftain's son who helped carry wood and water to the high-perched hermitage.

The boy was at first delighted, then apparently afraid. After all, it was a great adventure for a son of nomads who had never left his mountains except to take his family camels and goats to pasture, or to go on a trek to an oasis to trade hides for millet. A boy who had never smelled salt water might well hesitate about crossing the sea. First of all he had to get married to his childhood sweetheart, a step-sister. She was now 18 and he was almost 22. He could not marry her before he accompanied the family caravan to a place some 500 miles to the south, on the border of Nigeria, to bring back some scarce millet.

The expedition to France had to be postponed until the spring of 1913. Brother Charles sent out dozens of letters, most of them written on the backs of old envelopes, scraps of wrapping paper, whatever he could find. The letters outlined a formidable itinerary, designed to show Ouksem the real France, and were written to warn his prospective hosts not to be alarmed by the arrival of a blue-veiled warrior.

They visited his cousin Marie, who was summering with her grandchildren on the Atlantic beaches near Biarritz. The children were, no doubt, as much intrigued by the tight, well-buttered braids of the young man as he was fascinated by the gentle, white-haired surf of the Bay of Biscay.

The main course in Brother Charles' curriculum of French civilization for the young man was a sojourn with his sister Marie, her husband and their children at their chateau in Burgundy. Here Ouksem was exposed to the warm pleasures of a large and closely knit French family. He learned to ride a bicycle, an operation for which he had to tuck up the hem of his garment with safety pins.

July 27

PSALM 116:15   ISAIAH 25:6–9   HEBREWS 2:14–18

Brother Charles wanted Ouksem to teach the art of knitting to the women of his tribe, so he learned to knit while he was in France. He also learned a few words of French from Charles' nephew

Edward, and became adept at eating with a fork. Henri Laperrine, now General, thought that the young man should be able to compare his mountains of the Hoggar with the Alps, and he went with them to admire Mont Blanc and the Sea of Ice glacier. They crossed the Bernese Alps to Lucerne and re-entered France through the Jura mountains.

It was a real vacation for Brother Charles, and he was completely relaxed. He may have had a premonition that he would never see France again, that he was saying goodbye for the last time to his beloved cousin Marie, to his sister and her family, to his religious advisers, and to his old and dear friend Henri.

He was not in the least afraid of death. In fact, he had for years felt that being alive indicated his unworthiness to enter into the life everlasting. He had written a new will, specifying that he should be buried without a shroud or coffin at the exact spot of his death, and that his grave should be marked by no monument except a simple wooden cross.

As it had been for the past 20 years, his motto was still: 'Live as though you were to die today as a martyr.'

July 28

PSALM 102:8   PROVERBS 25:21–22   LUKE 6:27–36

In all his 15 years in Africa, Charles made not a single convert. One baby and one poor blind woman, who had no idea of what this new religion was about, had been baptized.

Times were hard, so he accumulated stores against a possible siege. The sacks of grain and flour, the tins of condensed milk and other food, the bolts of cloth and the supplies of medicines and sundry household objects were vast riches to people who sometimes did not eat two meals in a day. They were also a great temptation to the poor folk whom the priest had engaged to help in constructing his latest buildings.

One of these, El Madani, was a farmer of dubious honesty

whom the hermit had befriended ever since he first came there. He was caught stealing a bolt of calico from the storeroom. The corporal of engineers came over to superintend his punishment, and asked Brother Charles if he wished to have the man whipped there or sent away for 60 days' hard labour.

Brother Charles said, 'Let him go home. I gave him the cloth, Corporal. I promised it to his wife for a dress.' He put his arm on the farmer's shoulder. 'Go, my friend. Tell your wife to make a beautiful dress. I hope she enjoys it.'

When he had left, the corporal said, 'You're too good, Father. That man is a born thief and a no-good scoundrel. Everyone knows that he'll steal anything that's not nailed down.'

Brother Charles replied, 'He's a poor unfortunate wretch. He has been brought up in darkness. We do not love enough.'

The Corporal asked why he was so good to him. Brother Charles smiled sadly and replied, 'Didn't Jesus love Judas Iscariot?'

July 29

PSALM 89:1–2   JONAH 2:1–9   LUKE 22:39–46

> Then one of the twelve, who was called Judas Iscariot, went to the chief priests and said, 'What will you give me if I betray Him to you?' They paid him thirty pieces of silver. And from that moment he began to look for an opportunity to betray Him.
>
> *Matthew 26:14–16*

A group of Muslims from various fanatical sects and tribes hurried to meet El Madani, who knew the Christian Father and his routine. They knew that he could gain entrance to where Brother Charles was safely barricaded. His new quarters had walls two metres thick and a door reinforced with steel. El Madani demanded payment in cash – in silver.

Brother Charles passed these hours in solitary prayer. An earlier entry in his journal reads:

> What is our Lord doing in this last hour before His arrest, before His passion begins? He goes away alone to pray. So we, when we have severe trials to undergo, or some danger or some suffering to face, go aside to pray in solitude, and so pass the last hours that separate us from our trial.

July 30

PSALM 102:2   LAMENTATIONS 3:52–57   MARK 15:33–39

Brother Charles was alone. His freed servant, Paul, had served his supper. He had repeated the ominous rumours he had heard in the bazaar earlier in the day. An armed band had crossed the border and were riding unopposed in this direction, killing and pillaging along the way. There was even talk of a plot against the Father himself. He must make doubly sure that the door was bolted. Paul had then left and gone home to his wife and children, who lived in a hut about half a mile away.

Charles smiled tolerantly. Poor Paul! He would never be able to distinguish fact from fancy. Of course, he did throw the bolt as he closed the massive door. That was a matter of routine – not for himself, for he would still gladly darken the soil of Africa with his own blood, but for the protection of his parishioners in case of attack.

An attack seemed more remote than ever to Charles. When Paul had gone, he sat down to write his diary. Afterwards he spent some time in prayer and meditation at the foot of the blessed Sacrament, and then retired for the night.

His journal entry for December 1 1916 reads:

> It seems to me that we are in no danger at this moment. Our troops have been heavily reinforced. We have had no

serious new alert since September. The country is very calm.

He had barely finished writing when he was startled by an insistent pounding at the door. The pounding followed a pattern which he had instructed his parishioners to use in case of emergency. 'Who's there?' he called.

'Master! It is I – I bring the mail,' came the muffled reply.

Brother Charles thought that the voice was El Madani's. Perhaps the courier, behind schedule and in a hurry, had left letters with someone he knew was a friend of the Christian Father. El Madani was such a man... He slid back the bolt, twisted the heavy handle, drew back the door and held out one hand for the mail.

Instantly an iron grip was clamped about his wrist. He was dragged through the door with such force that he banged his head against the thick wall erected to protect the entrance from artillery and rifle fire. As he sank to his knees in an attitude of prayer, wild shrieks of victory were heard in the night. The muzzle of a rifle was jammed against the back of his head.

July 31 *Ignatius of Loyola*

PSALM 89:5–8   PROVERBS 14:32   PHILIPPIANS 1:21–23

A feeling of great elation welled up inside Charles' breast. The great desire of his African years, the wish to testify his faith with his own life, seemed about to be fulfilled.

The African who held the rifle to his head was only a boy – a lad of 13 or 14, perhaps only 12. He had been a toddler when the priest had first come. He knew him by name. His mother used to come to the hermitage for a handful of rice or millet to feed the boy during the drought...

Charles was scarcely aware that someone had tied his hands and feet. He was watching the men tramping in and out carrying the ammunition, the sacks of wheat, the crates of canned goods and the bolts of cloth. He scanned the faces, hoping he would recognize any of his friends. He did not see El Madani, although he was sure it was his voice that had prompted him to open the door.

A bearded Muslim chief hurled questions at the kneeling priest. Brother Charles said nothing. His lips moved, but no sound emerged. The chief wanted to know where the gold and silver were hidden. He said that everyone in the Sahara knew that the priest was a rich man. He should speak up if he valued his life.

The priest opened his eyes and smiled sadly, saying, 'I say to you, unless a grain of wheat falls into the ground and dies, it remains alone; but if it dies, it brings forth much fruit. He that loves his life, loses it, and he that hates his life in this world, shall keep it into everlasting life.'

At last Brother Charles caught sight of El Madani. He was one of three men escorting his servant Paul. They demanded that Paul tell them where the treasure was hidden, but he was too terrified to reply.

Suddenly there came the sound of camels and the click of rifle bolts, and the raiders fell silent and tried to take cover. The Arabs from the fort arrived and fired at the raiders. Instinctively Brother Charles stiffened and tried to rise to his feet. The boy behind him was seized with panic and pulled the trigger of his rifle. The sound was deadened because the muzzle was so close to the Christian Father's head. Brother Charles of Jesus sank back to his knees, slowly toppled to one side and rolled into the moat he had built to protect his poor parishioners in case of attack.

In 1897, 19 years before his death, he had written:

> Think that you may die a martyr, despoiled of everything, stretched on the ground, covered with blood and wounds, violently and painfully killed. Consider that such a death should be the object of your whole life; see in it how little other things matter. Think often of this death so as to be ready for it and to judge things at their true value in the light of it.

In 1914, however, he wrote to his cousin Marie:

> I cannot say I wish for death; I wished for it once; now I see
> so much good to be done, so many souls without a shep-
> herd.

August

JOURNEY THROUGH THE PSALMS

August 1

PSALM 84   DEUTERONOMY 6:4–6   MATTHEW 5:8

Blessed are those who have set their hearts on pilgrimage.

In our journey through the Psalms we will meet the full range of emotions: joy, pain, overflowing praise, anguish, trust, despair, bitterness, thankfulness. The Psalms give us permission to tell God we trust Him – but also to express our pain. 'How long? Why? When?' are frequent cries. How often do we encounter these desperate but real feelings in our hymns and worship songs? Crying out is allowed if the cry comes from the heart. This is where our journey must start: with a heart-cry, a longing for a movement closer to His courts, to the place where our life may begin to flow out from the very heart of God Himself. We cannot begin pilgrimage without this deep desire to seek God's face and heart, not primarily for what new blessing He can give us, but for who He is.

So we kneel and start tentatively on our journey. The road will, very likely, take us through dark and dry valleys. You cannot easily see out of a valley, but if our very being – soul, flesh, heart – is truly longing for the courts of the Lord, then we can take our first steps knowing that the path we have chosen is going in the right direction.

Heart of my own heart, whatever befall, still be my vision.

August 2

PSALM 19:7–14   EXODUS 3:1–3   LUKE 3:23A

Are we there yet?

One of the characteristics of today's society is that we expect
instant response to our demands. We press a button and expect
delivery. Now! But God loves us too much to allow those whose
hearts are steadfast to take short cuts. It is doubtful whether
Moses, growing up in a palace, had it in his plans to be a mere
shepherd in the desert – but where was it that God spoke to him?
The preparation times involved between God's call on our lives
and what the world, and sometimes the Church, classes as 'useful
activity' can feel interminable.

What counts in these times, when our feet are getting tired and
when everyone else seems to be passing us purposefully in the
fast lane, is where our thoughts are set. Are we content to keep
searching for the heart of God? How do we fill our minds in the
daily round – with complaint or contemplation?

May the words of my mouth and the meditation of my heart be
pleasing in Your sight.

August 3

PSALM 55:1–8, 16–18, 22   ISAIAH 41:8–10
    MATTHEW 14:28–30

If only I could fly, I would escape far away, and hide somewhere warm, somewhere safe.

I asked to be in Your presence, Lord, to sit at Your feet, to be surrounded by Your love. This really is my desire, Lord – I don't
think You heard me properly. The enemy is frightening me.

Where have You gone, God? I seem to spend my whole day crying out to You. How can I be useful if all I do is cry out?

Journeying in the dark can sometimes take on nightmare proportions. We know God is there, really. We have told dozens of others so, after all. So what has gone wrong? Why should it be that, soon after we set our hearts towards the throne room, the King appears to take a holiday?

Could it possibly be something to do with trust? Have we any idea yet what love the Father has lavished on us that He should answer our heart's cry?

But as for me, I trust in You.

August 4

PSALM 27   ISAIAH 41:13   2 CORINTHIANS 3:18

My heart says of You, 'Seek His face.' Your face, O Lord, I will seek.

Our age is one of the instant experience – we want it *now* and we want to *feel* it now. Many church songs today reflect this: 'I want...' 'Come now...' 'Hold me...' We must constantly ask ourselves whether we seek God's *face* or His *hands*. Is the one thing we ask 'to behold the beauty of the Lord' and so reflect it to others – or are we primarily after something else? Do we seek the giver or the gift?

Take heart, and wait for the Lord! His idea of time may be extremely frustrating, but we *will* see His goodness in the land of the living. We do not have to wait for the afterlife. There will be many more lessons in trust before we can claim confidently that we will not fear, even though an army may besiege us. Is trust not something to do with the greatness of our God? Once we start earnestly desiring Him, our journey takes us to those places which show us that our concept of God has just been too small.

God cannot be grasped with the mind. If He could be grasped, He would not be God.

Evagrius

August 5 *Oswald*

PSALM 25:4–5, 9–10   ISAIAH 55:8–9   HEBREWS 12:2–3

Somehow the journey does not seem to be progressing very quickly. We started with good intentions, but the light faded and the path became more winding, more hilly, more stony than anyone else's. In fact, it would seem that many of our Christian friends have now arrived at a river and have boarded a pleasure boat. They seem to be having a good time anyway. What is left for me? Surely not that old rowing boat lying in the weeds?

I think I mean it, Lord, when I say that I want to walk in Your paths, so I shall try not to write my own story. I will do what I can to look to You and You alone. Maybe You do want me to be laid aside for You? But I would still be happier doing something useful...

If He is truly our heart's desire, then we can never be satisfied until we stop struggling and humbly take the road which is sign-posted for us. If our desire is to know the heart of God, so as to pray out for our friends and neighbours, then we must be prepared to tread the path which will soften our hearts until we learn His compassion and weep with His tears.

August 6

PSALM 103:1–13   JEREMIAH 32:17   REVELATION 21:5

Praise the Lord, you His angels!
Praise the Lord, all His heavenly hosts!
Praise the Lord, all His works!
Praise the Lord, O my soul!

When our road seems rough and steep, hidden in mists or darkness, and we become tired, weary and downcast, then let us stop for a rest by the wayside and remember our journey so far. We have actually travelled further than we thought at first. Our travelling began, not with our decision to move closer to God, but with His love which does not treat our sins as we deserve – with the cross.

The process of being made new can often follow a path of pain. How *do* we pray when it hurts? How *do* we bless the Lord alongside the hosts of heaven? Sometimes we need to widen our vision, away from ourselves, for as soon as we place ourselves at the centre of the world, our vision becomes dangerously narrowed. We become so wrapped up in today's difficulties that we choose to forget the very fact of our great salvation, and we start seeking after so-called solutions – rather than seeking after the Father's heart.

> Jesus, You are changing me,
> as I let You reign supreme within my heart.

Marilyn Baker

August 7

PSALM 138   ISAIAH 46:9–10   PHILIPPIANS 1:6

The Lord will fulfil His purpose for me.

We can be sure of one thing: when God starts something, He will finish it properly. He does not begin a work in us only to go off elsewhere to start on someone else. He does not put us on the operating table and then leave in mid-operation. Yes, it might *feel* like that sometimes, but it is not what is actually happening.

So you think you took a wrong turning along the path? Or maybe you were going along all right until someone stood in the way with a 'DIVERSION' sign? Maybe you have arrived in a trackless desert, or at an apparent dead end. What now? Where is God in all this? How do we get back on the road?

God is God – the Lord. His roads do sometimes pass through deserts and over high walls. He also knows the way that we take. He is both behind us and before us. At the same time He is beside us, on our left and our right.

Though I walk in the midst of trouble, You preserve my life.

August 8

PSALM 51:6, 10–17   MALACHI 3:1–2   EPHESIANS 1:18

Our journey may have reached a not-very-scenic place for a reason. A desert, in particular, may not be welcome after the richness of the surroundings from which we have come. Yet it is in the featureless contexts of our travels that God can turn our eyes away from the view and on to the goal: His very presence. It is here that we begin to desire truth in the inmost place – a pure heart. So, trembling, we ask Him to purify our hearts. Often we have no idea of exactly what we are asking, but He who knows our hearts satisfies the deep desires of our hearts – even desires of which we are not yet aware.

It is costly to say, 'Come, Lord Jesus. Come, Holy Spirit.' Our God *is* a God who comes: to renew, to restore, to teach, to be alongside, to *purify*. Grant us a willing spirit, Lord.

> I know that the Immovable comes down; I know that the Invisible appears to me; I know He who is far outside the whole creation takes me within Himself and hides me in His arms.
>
> *St Symeon the New*

August 9

PSALM 13   ISAIAH 50:10–11   JOHN 1:5

How long, O Lord, how long?

The Psalms are honest: doubt and protest *are* allowed. Nonetheless, with the possible exception of one (Psalm 88), all the Psalms of pain, doubt and despair also express something of the Lord's greatness, love, compassion or salvation. We give voice both to our faith and to the real experience of our struggle to understand His ways. We must not worry that this is often a paradox. 'Lord, my way is hidden ... but today, I believe.'

We celebrate His presence together in worship, but He often seems absent. Psalm 88 ends with the words, 'the darkness is my closest friend'. How horrible, how desolate, that any of God's children, members of our family, those we dearly love, should be reduced to this. But wait – could this be true? Could the darkness actually be a friend? If so, we should not light our own torches.

We do not journey alone. Not everyone in the community of believers is in the same place at the same time. Alongside us there are people rejoicing, people despairing, those for whom God seems silent, those in darkness and those who are simply being bowled over by blessing. As a community, we must look out for others, 'each other's needs prefer'. If today's Psalm does not describe where I am just now, then it does give me an insight into how to pray for those around who are being broken by the waiting experience. Then, when I pray, I will be 'holding the Christ-light' for them.

> I watch you wait for the pain to go,
> I watch you wait for the love to flow
> I watch you wait for your heart to know healing.
> > *Iona, 'Healing', from the album* Beyond these Shores

August 10

PSALM 142   ISAIAH 30:15   PHILIPPIANS 3:10

Set me free from my prison, that I may praise Your name!

This Psalm is headed 'When David was in the cave'. We would, of course, prefer five-star hotels, with all expenses paid and full English breakfast, rather than caves. A cave is not exactly packed with comfort or entertainment. It is cold. Moreover, it is lonely. Prison walls can be lonely and cold, but they can take other shapes: self-pity, bitterness, anger, resentment. If our circumstances seem to us like a lonely cave or the walls of a prison, we can exhaust ourselves struggling against them, or we can wait for God inside them.

The Celtic saints, wandering for the love of Christ, interceding with a depth far beyond merely 'saying prayers', did not have access to central heating and duvets. They knew the power of Christ's resurrection – but they were also prepared to share in His sufferings. If we choose to tread along their paths, then we must also learn the art of cave-dwelling. We also need to learn to distinguish the difference between the refuge and the prison.

I cry to You, O Lord. I say, You are my refuge.

August 11   *Clare*

PSALM 42   AMOS 5:23–24   REVELATION 2:4

> As the deer pants for the water,
> so my soul longs after You,
> You alone are my heart's desire
> and I long to worship You.

Martin Nystrom

Here is a musician, one who has led the procession in the house of God, one who has been in the limelight, who has led worship on a grand scale. He is downcast, disturbed, oppressed and taunted. 'Where is your God?' they say to him. Where indeed? It is not just musicians who can get diverted away from their first love and enthusiasm for knowing Him more. Anyone who has an up-front role in their Christian community can easily be side-tracked, especially when God seems far away. The temptation is to put all your efforts into maintaining a good 'Christian' facade, when all the time you are crying inside and your heart is breaking.

This applies at two levels. First, for ourselves: it often takes quite drastic changes in our circumstances to make us realize that our heart's desire and what our lips are saying (or singing) are no longer one and the same. We have started to put conditions on worship; we use worship in a very self-centred way, for what we can get out of it. It no longer becomes a true outpouring from the love of our heart. Second, for others: somehow we have to understand how to live in love and vulnerability. It must be possible for anyone living in the kingdom to be free to express times of doubt and darkness without fear of being taunted or criticized. Who understands best the way through the mists? The one who has been that way before.

August 12

PSALM 130   I SAMUEL 10:8; 13:13–14   MATTHEW 13:44

My soul waits for the Lord.

'He himself will redeem Israel from all their sins.' Psalm 49 tells us that no one can redeem the life of another. We get impatient and frustrated, not just in waiting for God to act in our own situations, but also as we await answers for those we love. It sometimes breaks us up – watching, suffering. If only... Why does God not come and *do* something? It is as though He sits in the sky twiddling His thumbs. We feel we must do something ourselves if God will not rouse Himself.

If the Lord of heaven is at work in us, answering our cry to be in His presence, then there are no short cuts. Why did the man who found the treasure in the field not simply go and dig it up one night when nobody was looking? Why did he bother to buy the whole field? Cheating devalues the treasure. So we learn, slowly, to wait in trust – for ourselves and for those we uphold in prayer. It's hard, isn't it?

> Thou and Thou only the first in my heart
> High King of heaven, my treasure Thou art.
> *Ancient Irish, translated by Mary Byrne*

August 13

PSALM 63:1–8   ISAIAH 43:18–19   JOHN 13:7

Earnestly I seek you.

When our seeking moves to earnest seeking, when we begin to see that God is indeed GOD, when we thirst and long for Him, when we sing in the shadow of His wings and cling to Him, then streams can begin to flow in the desert. The desert itself may not change, but our view of it does.

It is true that some deserts are caused by our wilful and deliberate sin, and no amount of complaining and distress calls to the Most High will change the need for repentance and obedience. We cannot, however, always discern why our journey has arrived in a dry and weary land.

At first we expend energy desperately trying to escape – filling our prayer time asking for green pastures and still waters. We can become so absorbed with exaggerated memories of these pleasant places, so immersed in our desire to leave the dry place, that we miss seeing the trickle of water that has just emerged right where we are. Our God does provide water in the desert – not necessarily choice wine, but life-giving water. Let us not fail to recognize the water of life because we have our hearts set on the wine of past places.

August 14

PSALM 36:5–9   SONG OF SONGS 2:4   MATTHEW 5:6

You give them drink from Your river of delights.

The Psalms are not entirely filled with cries of protest and despair when God seems absent. There is much joy and hope within their pages. There will be times for us when the healing streams *do* flow. Nothing can prevent His love and faithfulness towards each one of us; nothing can plug this fountain of life to stop it flowing. We can move away from it so as not to get wet. We can go to the banquet and politely eat a dry biscuit in the corner, because we do not trust the rich fare set before us, or do not consider ourselves worthy. Yet this sort of behaviour will not enable us to see things in the light of God.

There are two very important lessons to be learned from this 'oasis' Psalm. First, there are no favourites in the kingdom: it is for both high and low to find refuge, and to feast and drink from the abundant love of God. When the wind blows, everyone who is out in the open will feel it, unless they have chosen shelter. When God breathes His Spirit on His people, He does not exclude any who have chosen to be open. Second, 'In Your light, we see light': only by His illumination can we see the truth of our situation. We can shine our pathetic little torches, analyse and agonize, but in the end we may only really see light on the other side of the desert when we look back and realize that we have been guided all along – but via paths that did not appear on our map.

Christ as a light, illumine and guide me.

August 15 Mary, mother of Jesus

PSALM 3   2 CHRONICLES 20:21–22   MATTHEW 5:7

May God arise, let His enemies be scattered, may His foes flee before Him!

If we set out to make the Psalms part of our lives, to pray out from them, to worship with them, to recite them as companions on the road, then it will not be long before we arrive at verses we find difficult. What should we make of the attitude of the psalmists concerning the wicked? There are, quite honestly, some very difficult sentiments, and some of the curses expressed are repugnant to us.

We have to be clear just who the enemy is – then we can join battle in the right place with the right weapons. We know that our struggle is not against flesh and blood, but against principalities and powers. We know that the weapons we fight with are not the weapons of the world, for our weapons are designed to demolish strongholds in people's lives, not the people themselves. Certainly, the Christian pilgrimage is going to take us to places where we encounter the enemy. True pilgrims go with the shield of the Lord round about them and the authority to speak out against the real enemy. They also show compassion and discernment, so that people enslaved by evil are blessed rather than destroyed by words of power.

Abba Poeman said:

> If I am in a place where there are enemies, I
> become a soldier.

The Sayings of the Desert Fathers

August 16

PSALM 122   JEREMIAH 29:7   MATTHEW 5:9

May the peace of the Lord Christ go with you, wherever He may send you.

Sometimes our journeys take us to places which are not technically deserts or dead ends, but places where our souls do not easily find rest, surroundings where we do not feel we belong, places we just do not feel able to relate to spiritually. These are not necessarily places of spiritual darkness, just somewhere we cannot call 'home'.

It is easier to pray for the peace of our Jerusalem – that place where we feel nearest to heaven, that place where we rejoice to go and worship. It is a much harder thing to pray for the peace of the place of exile. That is what it can sometimes feel like. Exile can stifle our song. 'How could we sing the Lord's song in a foreign land?' (Psalm 137:4) In exile, as in the desert, we may experience bitterness and resentment. If we cannot sing, we must at least *pray* for the place of exile. It has much to teach us. We even have a part in its spiritual prosperity.

> O Lord, grant me to greet the coming day in peace.
> Direct my will, teach me to pray, pray Thou Thyself in me.
> *Metropolitan Philaret of Moscow*

August 17

PSALM 131   EXODUS 16:1–3   ACTS 9:1–2, 10

I have stilled my soul.

> The Christian's greatest struggle is the struggle not to struggle.
> *Arthur Burt*

While we are protesting and complaining in exile, misremembering times past and living in a fantasy future, we are not being consistent concerning our heart-cry. Our lips may have sought the face of the Lord, but our hearts are still imposing conditions. It is only when we can reach a point of stillness before God that we can start to see what is around us from His perspective.

We are part of the body of Christ. Our stories overlap with others' stories. We can be so self-centred in trying to see what He is doing in our lives, that we can miss the way this process can be part of the story of another saint. The Lord can only call to us in visions if we are prepared for them to catapult us along paths we have never dreamed of, paths which sometimes seem just a little steep. We long to see more clearly and follow more nearly – but to what end? That we may enjoy an 'experience' – or that we may in some way be a stepping stone for someone else's journey through a muddy patch?

> Breathe on me, breath of God,
> until my heart is pure;
> until my will is one with Thine.

Edwin Hatch

August 18

PSALM 18:1–3, 16–19   PROVERBS 15:17   HEBREWS 13:1–2

He brought me out into a spacious place. He rescued me because He delighted in me.

We can probably all think of spacious places we have known along our journeys so far. There may be places where we feel especially close to heaven – Lindisfarne or Iona, for example, somewhere which has been fashioned not only by our Creator God, but where there is a special continuity of the communion of saints through the ages. Most of us cannot be there all the time, however, nor would we want to be. There may be other places – retreat houses, homes – which have become special to us, places where we have been restored by new hope, new vision, in an atmosphere of acceptance and love.

What about our own rooms, our own homes, however dark or small they may be, whether set in beautiful countryside or in the midst of decaying cities? Could these, too, become spacious places for a fellow traveller, places filled with prayer, beacons of light in dark streets, places of refuge along the way? Hospitality is more than just bed and cornflakes. Indeed, some of us have neither the extra bed nor funds for the cornflakes. Nonetheless, if we eagerly desire it, and seek to be closer to the heart of God, we can perhaps provide an armchair of love, even at those times when we feel that we ourselves are in difficulties.

The important thing is to be open to the idea of *being* that place of blessing, even when we so much desire to *be in* a place of blessing ourselves.

One of the Fathers said:

> I have seen four orders in heaven: in the first order
> is the sick man who gives thanks to God; in the
> second, the man who observes hospitality and for
> that reason gets up to serve; in the third, the man
> who crosses the desert without seeing anyone; in
> the fourth, the man who obeys his Father and
> remains in submission to him for the Lord's sake.
> *The Sayings of the Desert Fathers*

August 19

PSALM 34:1–8, 18   JEREMIAH 31:21A   MATTHEW 5:3

Let us exalt His Name together.

Well-trodden paths are the easiest to follow. We know how bewildering it can be walking up on the moors. We start from the pasture, or maybe a well-defined green lane. The signpost is clear. We walk with confidence and enthusiasm. Then, all of a sudden, the landscape changes and we find ourselves in bog or bracken, with no sign of a footpath and only disinterested sheep for company.

If we are walking through places with undefined paths, where we cannot see the destination, then it is wise to take note of our journey and set up waymarks – because one day these may be of help to someone else heading in the same direction. It is also good to see just where we have come from and how far on we are. Sometimes we do not realize that we have made any progress at all! Often it takes someone else to point it out to us. No two journeys are the same, but the terrain may at least be similar.

It is hardly likely that the psalmists had any idea that these songs, these outpourings in song of their experiences, would still be assisting the journeyings of the people of God so many centuries later.

Taste and see that the Lord is good!

August 20   Oswin

PSALM 31:14–16, 19–24   JOB 42:10   MATTHEW 5:10

My times are in Your hands.

The psalmist has just lamented that he is consumed by anguish, and even his friends avoid him. He is an object of dread to them, and they pass by on the other side. Those around him have been whispering, slandering.

What do we do, how do we react, when those we feel should be supporting us seemingly give up on us, or, like Job's 'friends', come full of advice and criticism, but not much in the way of love? People around us want our life circumstances to look less messy, more normal, more acceptable and successful. We embarrass our friends, who want us to be normal again. We know our times are indeed in the hands of the Lord – but that does not necessarily prevent us from feeling trapped, as though in a besieged city.

When we feel cornered and pressured like this, we have the choice of being aggressive and seeking retribution, or of taking refuge in God our fortress and from there praying for both our friends and our enemies. Rather than instruct God on how best to change these people so that they start to conform to our own will, we need to speak out prayers of blessing.

Where do these prayers come from at such a time? How do we pray for others when they are hurting us? Become immersed in these Psalms! Pray them out, not just for ourselves, but for those around us. And pray from the safety and protection of the shadow of His wings.

August 21

PSALM 119:164–176   DANIEL 6:10   I THESSALONIANS 5:23–24

Seven times a day I praise You.

This verse is at the root of the Divine Office: Lauds, Matins, Vespers, Terce, Sext, None, Prime and Compline. (That's eight times, yes, but the development of the Office is another story!) In the early Middle Ages, the whole Psalter would be recited every week and it was assumed that the monks would know it by heart. The Psalms have always been the driving energy of the Office. As we absorb them, day by day, phrase by phrase, they can become part of the sinew and tissue of our lives, building us up to be warriors of God.

They show a deepening in prayer for oneself and in prayer for others. They both nourished and expressed the prayer of the people of God. Their prayer is inseparably personal and communal. Their prayer recalls the saving events of the past, yet extends into the future. The Psalter's many forms of prayer take shape both in the liturgy of the temple and in the human heart. The prayer of the Psalms is always sustained by praise.

From the Catechism of the Catholic Church

May my lips overflow with praise, for You teach me Your decrees.

August 22

PSALM 86:1–13   PROVERBS 4:23   MATTHEW 5:8

Give me an undivided heart.

No one but You, Lord, can satisfy the longing of my heart. Nothing I do, Lord, can take the place of drawing near to You.

Andy Park

This kind of heart surgery takes time. We get bored with all the waiting, the times which seem, in comparison to our busy and productive pasts, so unfruitful, so barren. We used to be Important; we were known for what we did; we were labelled according to our role. Now we hear, 'What do you do all day?' How we long to be able to reply with a catalogue of great achievements, tangible results, solid successes – anything at all that would be obvious and presentable.

It is, once again, the temptation of the short cut. It is not that our lives are unfruitful simply because we are not busy *doing*. Fruit, in any case, is seasonal. In the community of believers, some are bearing visible fruit, while others are shedding their leaves. What counts is that the tree is rooted and grounded in the love of God, planted by streams of water.

Abba Poeman said:

> Do not give your heart to that which does not
> satisfy your heart.
>
> *The Sayings of the Desert Fathers*

August 23

PSALM 23   PROVERBS 25:20   PHILIPPIANS 4:12–14

He restores my soul.

We know full well that our journey will not be through green pastures for ever. If we are serious about following Jesus, then we must often follow Him through the darkness, through the valley. On a sunny, warm day out in the country, it is hard to imagine what it is like to be cold, or to be enclosed by the city. We forget so quickly, though memories assure us of the reality. Not everyone journeys to the same place at the same time, however: some are in darkness while others are in light; some are in the valleys while others are on the hilltops; some are in pasturelands while others are in the desert.

We need to recognize the valid experiences of those in the opposite places from where we are just now. We need to do our best to remember something of what those experiences meant for us when we were there (if indeed we have ever been there ourselves), and also to see that the kingdom is so big that no two places are the same! How should we pray for those in the valleys? Well, one of the reasons for our determination to seek the face of God must surely be to assist us in intercession, so that our prayers come from a heart of brokenness and not from a position of superiority.

We need to learn to hold the Christ-light for others, but, if necessary, we need also to be willing for them to walk on past us, perhaps along a path other than the one we have allocated for them in the assumed wisdom of our own prescriptive prayers.

> I will hold the Christ-light for you
> in the night-time of your fear.
>
> *Richard Gillard, 'The Servant Song'*

August 24

PSALM 66   ISAIAH 57:15   JOHN 4:6

If I had cherished sin in my heart, the Lord would not have listened.

Jesus' question to the man at the pool seems absurd. How do you even conceive of asking someone who has been ill for 38 years whether they want to get well? But wait, examine your own heart for a moment. It is possible that you are cherishing something which is a real impediment to your progress, but which nevertheless gives you sympathy, or attention, or an identity. The man at the pool had to ask himself, 'Would people still bother with me if I didn't seem to have any problems, if my healing made me more "normal", less unusual?'

We have a responsibility beyond ourselves to allow God to stir the waters in our secret lives and to lay aside our need to be carried all the time. Whether or not we feel accepted and loved by the rest of the Body of Christ, we are still part of that Body. If we are not functioning as we should be, then other parts of the Body are hindered and put under strain. We *must* be stirred if we are to experience the miracle.

Do you remember the dwarfs in C. S. Lewis' book *The Last Battle*? They were in a prison of their own making, and would not dare to leave it in order to go 'higher up and further in'. Here is what Aslan says about them: 'They will not let us help them. They have chosen cunning instead of belief. Their prison is only in their minds, yet they are in that prison; and so afraid of being taken in that they cannot be taken out.'

Can we dare to trust Him? Yes! He does not deceive us. He will not withhold His love from us.

August 25 *Ebba*

PSALM 107:1–16   ISAIAH 43:1–4   EPHESIANS 3:17B–19

> Jesu, Thou art all compassion,
> pure unbounded love Thou art.
> Visit us with Thy salvation,
> enter every trembling heart.

Charles Wesley

Unfailing love. Unlimited, unbounded love.

> Set our hearts on fire with love to Thee, O Christ our God, that in its flame we may love Thee with all our heart, with all our mind, with all our soul and with all our strength, and our neighbours as ourselves, so that, keeping Thy commandments, we may glorify Thee the Giver of all good gifts.

Kontakion

> O Thou who camest from above,
> the pure celestial fire to impart,
> kindle a flame of sacred love
> on the mean altar of my heart.

Charles Wesley

August 26 Ninian

PSALM 139:1–12, 23–24   I SAMUEL 16:7   MATTHEW 6:21

Search me, O God, and know my heart.

To a certain extent, we are all able to search and know our own
hearts. There are hidden things which God will reveal at the right
time and in the right place if we mean business with Him. Yet
sometimes we make excuses for not facing up to what we know is
already there: some hindrance to our moving on. If we choose to
bury these things deeper, we do not fool God, who has searched
us and knows us. We do not even fool many of those closest to us.
We only fool ourselves.

When we face up to the things which we know need cleansing
and bring them to His heart of love, He does not turn round and
say, 'And what do you expect Me to do about *that*?' No, He alone
can cleanse hearts thoroughly. His power is as great as His love.

> Almighty God,
> to whom all hearts are open,
> all desires known,
> and from whom no secrets are hidden:
> cleanse the thoughts of our hearts
> by the inspiration of Your Holy Spirit,
> that we may perfectly love You,
> and worthily magnify Your holy Name;
> through Christ our Lord. Amen.
>
> The Alternative Service Book 1980,
> *Order for Holy Communion Rite A*

August 27

PSALM 116   HABAKKUK 3:17–18   PHILIPPIANS 3:8

Here is a Psalm from the far side of the wilderness: 'Be at rest once more, my soul, for the Lord has been good to you.' Good? This desolation is good? It is rare that, in the midst of darkness, we can feel deep inside that the process is for the good; not only for our own good, but even for the glory of His Name, for the furthering of the kingdom of God, as our broken lives and softer hearts touch those we pass. Am I prepared to trust God through the barren time, when all I once held dear is being stripped away? 'Break me, melt me, mould me, fill me.' I would be happy with just the filling, if You don't mind, Lord: please miss out the rest!

> I have never met anyone in a desert who can possibly believe God will ever use them again! Probably we could all accept our deserts far more easily if we could see them in the context of our whole lives. The most trying part of spiritual deserts is that at the time we never realize their significance.
>
> *Jennifer Rees Larcombe,* Where Have You Gone, God?

O Love that wilt not let me go,
I rest my weary soul in Thee;
I give Thee back the life I owe,
that in Thine ocean depths its flow
may richer, fuller be.

O Joy that seekest me through pain,
I cannot close my heart to Thee:
I trace the rainbow through the rain,
and feel the promise is not vain
that morn shall tearless be.

George Matheson

August 28 Pelagius

PSALM 96   LAMENTATIONS 3:22–23   REVELATION 5:12–14

Worship the Lord in the beauty of holiness.

There is a time when we should cease to pore over the map and
take in the scenery instead. I know someone who will walk for
miles to a viewpoint in the middle of nowhere. What does he do
on arrival? Rather than enjoying the view, he sticks his head in
the map! It may be interesting or even essential to see where we
have come from and where we think we are going next, but this
must never be at the expense of learning to *be* where we are, to
enjoy the beauty of the moment.

There is a sense in which worship is a journey. We enter the
gates, go through the courts and approach the holy place. Many of
the Psalms were used on the physical journey up to the temple at
great festivals. It is also true, however, that too much concern
about the journey itself deflects us from our desire to worship.
What is worship? It is the outflow of a heart that loves God and
enjoys God.

> Low at His feet lay thy burden of carefulness;
> high on His heart He will bear it for thee,
> comfort thy sorrows and answer thy prayerfulness,
> guiding thy steps as may best for thee be.

> *J. S. B. Monsell*

August 29

PSALM 119:65–72   ISAIAH 7:7–8   EPHESIANS 5:19

Teach me knowledge and good judgement.

For the monks of old, the Psalms were not just to travel *through*, picking out bits here and there for comfort and solace. Their journeying was not so much through the Psalms as *with* the Psalms. Psalms were recited aloud, frequently – inside, outside, on the move, in stillness, in community, alone. They were painstakingly written out. They were memorized – presumably even Psalm 119! We think we do not need to learn the Psalms today. We all have copies, in different versions to suit our moods, and indexes and concordances to help us find the 'nice' bits. But would it not be worth having these words written on our hearts?

> The life of Aidan is in marked contrast to the apathy of our own times, for all who walked with him, whether monks or layfolk, were required to meditate, that is, either to read the Scriptures or to learn the Psalms. This was their daily occupation wherever they went.
>
> *Bede*

> I eat little, and sleep little. When I eat I continue praying, and when I sleep my snores are songs of praise.
>
> *A Celtic monk*

August 30

PSALM 73:21–28   PROVERBS 17:3   HEBREWS 12:15

When my heart was grieved and my spirit embittered, I was a brute beast before You.

Bitterness, once rooted, is a deadly poison. It not only undermines relationships and renders churches ineffective, but, unchecked, it can grow inside a person and choke them. Who is it that tests the heart? Many of us have sung the words, 'Refiner's fire, my heart's one desire is to be holy.' One great refining is to recognize bitterness taking root, and to be willing for it to be dealt with. We must learn to be a people who do not foster its growth through gossip, mutterings and murmurings, which can only cause factions and rifts.

If you really are serious about the growth of your heart, then you are almost guaranteed to meet this particular refinement fairly early on, for no one can minister the love of God with an embittered spirit.

> Abba Lot went to see Abba Joseph and said to him, 'Abba, as far as I can, I say my little Office, I fast a little, I pray and meditate, I live in peace and as far as I can, I purify my thoughts. What else can I do?' Then the old man stood up and stretched his hands towards heaven. His fingers became like ten lamps of fire and he said to him, 'If you will, you can become all flame.'
>
> *The Sayings of the Desert Fathers*

> Make my heart to grow as great as Thine,
> so through my hurt Your love may shine.
>
> *From* Saranam

August 31 Aidan

PSALM 18:25–36, 46   DEUTERONOMY 33:12
PHILIPPIANS 3:12–14

> Advancing on the way, each one finds that God grows ever more intimate and ever more distant, well known and yet unknown. God dwells in light unapproachable, yet man stands in His presence with loving confidence and addresses Him as friend. God is both end-point and starting-point. He is the host who welcomes us at the conclusion of the journey, yet He is also the companion who walks by our side every step upon the way.
>
> *Kallistos Ware,* The Orthodox Way

Everyone who thinks he has arrived at his destination has actually hardly begun, and he who continues searching is closer to his destination than he realizes.

Dave Tomlinson, The Post Evangelical

Where our thoughts of Him end, there He begins.

September

SAYINGS OF THE DESERT FATHERS

This month's readings are sayings of the Desert Fathers and Mothers (or Abbas and Ammas), the very first monks and nuns. They fled into the deserts of Egypt, Palestine and Syria, starting with St Antony at the end of the third century. They wanted a life of solitude in which to seek God for His own sake and live out their Christian faith away from the pressures and temptations of the world. Yet they also sought each other's help and advice, because they recognized that in solitude and quiet we are forced to confront the sin and temptation that lie within.

Their collective wisdom and understanding was seen as being so helpful that their sayings and stories were gathered into books very early on. These sayings, and the lives and spirituality out of which the sayings grew, has had a great influence throughout the centuries – on the Celtic Church, on the Western and (especially) Eastern Churches, on our own Northumbria Community, and on Christian theology in general.

September 1

PSALM 23:1–3   JEREMIAH 15:16–17   MARK 6:30–31

> Amma Matrona said, 'It is better to be surrounded by many people and to choose the solitary life, than to be alone, and for your mind to be filled with the desire to be one with the crowd.'

September 2

PSALM 23:4   I KINGS 19:3–5A   LUKE 22:39–43

A certain brother came to Abba Moses in Scete seeking a word from him. And the old man said to him, 'Go and sit in your cell, and your cell shall teach you everything.'

A brother came to see a very experienced old man and said to him, 'I am in trouble.' The old man replied, 'Sit in your cell and God will give you peace.'

September 3

PSALM 23:5–6   I KINGS 19:5B–8   LUKE 18:9–14

One of the Fathers told a story of a certain elder who was in his cell busy at work and wearing a hairshirt when Abba Ammonas came to him. When Abba Ammonas saw him wearing a hairshirt he said, 'That thing won't do you a bit of good.'

The elder replied, 'Three thoughts are troubling me. The first impels me to withdraw somewhere in the wilderness. The second, to seek a foreign land where no one knows me. The third, to wall myself into this cell, and see no one, and eat only every second day.'

Abba Ammonas said to him, 'None of these three will do you a bit of good. But rather sit in your cell, eat a little every day, and have always in your heart the words which are read in the Gospel and were said by the tax-collector: *Lord Jesus Christ, Son of the living God, have mercy on me, a sinner*. Thus you can be saved.'

This phrase from Luke 18:13 is the basis of the 'Jesus Prayer', repeated over and over in the Eastern Orthodox tradition.

September 4

PSALM 27:7–11B   I KINGS 19:9–13   ROMANS 12:10–11

> The brethren asked the Abba Poemen about a certain brother who would fast for six days out of the seven with perfect abstinence, but always seemed ill-tempered. And the old man gave answer, 'He has taught himself to fast for six days but not to control his temper. It would be better for him to bring greater zeal to the task which should be less hard work!'

> Abba Antony said, 'There are some who wear out their bodies with abstinence; but because they have no discretion, they are far away from God, and His ways.'

Discretion is the ability to discern what is good and right and of God, both in me and in what goes on around me. It was a key spiritual ability sought by the Desert Fathers through faith, prayer and spiritual exercise. Often the Lord gives it as sheer gift.

Our spiritual routine should help us to seek God and His will in our lives. It should never distract or divert us from seeking Him.

September 5 *Teresa of Calcutta*

PSALM 19:14   PROVERBS 10:19–20; 29:11   JAMES 1:19–21

> Abba Macarius said, 'If, wishing to correct another, you are moved to anger, you gratify your own passion. Do not lose yourself in order to save another.'

> Abba Hyperichius observed, 'A monk who cannot hold his tongue when he is angry will not be able to control the passion of lust, either.'

It was said of Abba Agatho that for three years he carried a stone in his mouth until he learned to be silent.

Do not talk, unless you can improve on silence.

September 6

PSALM 9:7–10   EXODUS 34:6–7A   MATTHEW 7:1–5

Abba Joseph asked Abba Pastor, 'Tell me how I can become a monk.'

The elder replied, 'If you want to have rest here in this life and also in the next, in every conflict with another say: *Who am I?* and so judge no one.'

A brother in Scete happened to commit a fault, and the elders assembled and sent for Abba Moses to join them. He, however, did not want to come.

The priest sent him a message, saying, 'Do come: the community of the brethren is waiting for you.'

So he arose and started off. And taking with him a very old basket full of holes, he filled it with sand and carried it behind him. The elders came out to meet him and said, 'What is this, Father?'

Abba Moses replied, 'My sins are running out behind me and I do not see them – and today I come to judge the sins of another!'

They, hearing this, said nothing to the brother but pardoned him.

Abba Moses also said, 'A man ought to be like a dead man with his companion, since to die to one's friend is to cease to judge him in anything.'

September 7

PSALM 4:4–8   ECCLESIASTES 7:8–9   EPHESIANS 4:26–27, 30–32

A hesychast is someone who pursues a life of inner stillness and quiet in order to listen to God with a heart open to receive Him and His will.

> There was one brother who was a hesychast in a monastery, but he often got angry. So he said within himself, 'I will go and live apart, alone, and the fact of having nothing to do with anyone will assuage this passion of mine.' So he went away and lived in solitude in a cave.
>
> Now one day when he had filled his jug with water he put it on the ground and suddenly it fell over. He picked it up, filled it, and it fell over again. Having filled it a third time, he put it down and it fell over again. He was furious and picked it up and broke it. Coming to his senses, he recognized that he had been deceived by the enemy and he said, 'Since I have been overcome, even after withdrawing into solitude, I will go back to the monastery, for everywhere there is warfare, endurance, and the help of God.'
>
> So he arose and returned to his place.

September 8

PSALM 133:1–3   PROVERBS 17:9   COLOSSIANS 3:12–14

> Abba Macarius said, 'If we dwell upon the harms that have been done to us by people, we amputate from our mind the power of dwelling upon God.'

September 9

PSALM 25:8–11   NUMBERS 14:19–20   MATTHEW 18:21–35

It happened that temptation fell upon a brother in the monastery of Abba Elias and they threw him out: and he came to the mountain, to Abba Antony. After he had been with him for some time, Antony sent him back to the community he had come from.

But when they saw him, they again drove him away: and again he made his way to the Abba Antony, saying, 'They would not receive me, Father.'

Then the old man sent to them, saying, 'A ship was wrecked at sea, and lost all the cargo that it carried, and with hard toil was the empty ship brought at last to land. Is it your wish to sink on land the ship that has returned safe from the sea?'

And they recognized that it was the Abba Antony who had sent him back; and straightaway they took him in.

September 10

PSALM 25:14   ZECHARIAH 7:8–13   I CORINTHIANS 10:23–24

According to Abba John the Eunuch, Abba Antony once said, 'I have never put my own convenience before the benefit of my brother.'

'Have mercy on all,' said Abba Pambo, 'for mercy leads to freedom of speech before God.'

September 11

PSALM 8:1, 3–5, 9   ISAIAH 14:13–15   2 THESSALONIANS 3:6–15

For by the grace given to me I say to everyone among you not to think of yourself more highly than you ought to think, but to think with sober judgement, each according to the measure of faith that God has assigned.

Romans 12:3

An interesting story is told about Abba John Colobos (also often referred to as 'John the Dwarf'). At that time he shared the cell of another brother in order to learn by his example. One day he said to his brother, 'I want to live in the same security as the angels have, doing no work, but serving God without any distraction or interruption.' And casting off everything he had on, he started out into the desert.

When a week had gone by he returned to his brother. And while he was knocking on the door, his brother called out before opening, and asked, 'Who are you?'

He replied, 'I am John.'

Then his brother answered and said, 'John has become an angel and is no longer among us.'

But John kept on knocking and said, 'It is I.'

Still the brother did not open, but kept him waiting. Finally, opening the door, he said, 'If you are a man, you are going to have to start working again in order to live. But if you are an angel, what possible reason would you have to come inside my cell?'

So John did penance and said, 'Forgive me, brother, for I have sinned.'

September 12

PSALM 34:1–10   DANIEL 3:28   I CORINTHIANS 13:1–3

A brother asked one of the elders, saying, 'There are two brothers, of whom one remains praying in his cell, fasting six days at a time and doing a great deal of penance. The other one takes care of the sick. Which one's work is more pleasing to God?'

The elder replied, 'If that brother who fasts six days at a time were to hang himself up by the nose, he could not equal the one who takes care of the sick.'

Lord, please keep me from being so heavenly minded that I am of no earthly use to You.

September 13

PSALM 145:17–19   DEUTERONOMY 4:7   MATTHEW 11:28–30

A brother questioned an old man, saying, 'My thoughts wander and I am troubled by this.'

The old man said to him, 'Remain sitting in your cell and your thoughts will come to rest. For truly, just as when the she-ass is tied her colt runs here and there but always comes back to his mother wherever she is, so it is with the thoughts of him who for God's sake remains steadfast in his cell: even if they wander a little, they will always come back to him.'

September 14

PSALM 86:11–13   JEREMIAH 29:11–14A   COLOSSIANS 3:1–4

A brother came to Abba Pastor and said, 'Many distracting thoughts come into my mind, and I am in danger because of them.'

Then the elder thrust him out into the open air and said, 'Open up your garments about your chest and catch the wind in them.'

But he replied, 'This I cannot do.'

So the elder said to him, 'If you cannot catch the wind, neither can you prevent distracting thoughts from coming into your head. Your job is to say, No, to them.'

One of the elders said, 'Pray attentively and your thoughts will soon straighten out.'

September 15

PSALM 51:1–6   EXODUS 20:20   I CORINTHIANS 10:12–13

A brother asked one of the Fathers if a person is defiled by having evil thoughts. There was a discussion on the subject, and some said, Yes, that person is defiled, and others, No, or else – poor men that we are – we could not be saved; what counts is not to carry them out in practice. The brother went to a very experienced old man to question him about the discussion. The old man said to him, 'What is required of each one is regulated according to his capacity.'

The brother begged the old man to explain, saying, 'For the Lord's sake, explain this saying.'

The old man said to him, 'Suppose a tempting object is placed here and two brothers, of whom one is more advanced in virtue than the other, come in. He who is perfect says to himself, "I should very much like to have this object," but he does not rest in this thought; he cuts it off at once and he is not defiled. But if he who has not yet come to this measure desires the object and his thought clings to it – still if he does not take it – he also is not defiled.'

September 16

PSALM 51:7–12   ZECHARIAH 3:1–4   JAMES 4:7–8

A brother asked an old man, 'What shall I do, for the temptations which war against me are many and I do not know how to fight against them?'

The old man said to him, 'Do not fight against all of them, but against only one, for all a monk's temptations have one single head. So it is against this head that one must be on guard, and fight; and thus all temptations diminish.'

Concerning evil thoughts, the same old man replied, 'My brothers, I entreat you, just as we have cut out deeds, so let us cut out desires also.'

September 17

PSALM 51:13–17   DEUTERONOMY 8:2–5   JAMES 1:2–5

Abba Pastor said that Abba John the Dwarf had prayed to the Lord, and the Lord had taken away all his passions, so that he became able to resist any temptation. And in this condition he went to one of the elders and said, 'You see before you a man who is completely at rest and has no more temptations.'

The elder said, 'Go and pray to the Lord to command some struggle to be stirred up in you, for the soul is matured only in battles.'

He did so. Then when the temptations started up again he did not pray that the struggle be taken away from him, but only said, 'Lord, give me strength to get through the fight.'

September 18

PSALM 1:1–3   EZEKIEL 47:1, 12   HEBREWS 10:24–25

An old man said, 'Just as a tree cannot bring forth fruit if it is always being transplanted, so the monk who is always going from one place to another is not able to bring forth virtue.'

September 19

PSALM 34:11–14   PROVERBS 17:14   I CORINTHIANS 13:4–7

There were two old men living together in one cell and never had there risen even the paltriest contention between them. So the one said to the other, 'Let us have one quarrel the way other men do.'

But the other said, 'I do not know how to make a quarrel.'

The first said, 'Look, I'll put a tile down between us and say, "That is mine" and then you have to say, "It is not yours, it's mine." And then that causes contention and it turns into a squabble.'

So they set the tile between them and the first one said, 'That is mine' and the second made reply, 'I hope that it is mine.' And the first said, 'It is not yours: it's mine.'

To which the second made answer, 'If it's yours, take it.' And after that they could find no way of quarrelling.

September 20

PSALM 62:5–8   ISAIAH 40:27–31   I THESSALONIANS 4:16–18

A brother questioned one of the Fathers, saying, 'If I happen to be overcome by sleep and miss the proper time for gathering to say office, I am afraid of what people will think, and I no longer want to say the prayers if I have to say them late.'

The old man said to him, 'If it happens that you are drowsy and sleep through till next morning, then get up, shut your door and your window and say your office. For truly it is written: *The day is Yours and the night is Yours also*. In truth, God is glorified at all times.'

Wake up from your sleep,
rise from the dead,
and Christ will shine upon you.

It is better to do the Office late than not at all, because it provides us with anchors through the day, bringing us back to God in the midst of everything else that crowds in on us.

An old man said, 'Having arisen in the early hours, say to yourself, "Body, you must work to feed yourself; soul, be vigilant in order to receive your inheritance."'

September 21 *Henri Nouwen*

PSALM 145:14   PROVERBS 28:13   JAMES 5:16

A brother was attacked by lust, and the warfare was like a burning fire in his heart, day and night. The brother fought so as not to consent to these thoughts. After a long time the attacks ceased, unable to gain any ground because of the brother's endurance; then immediately a light came into his heart.

Another brother was attacked by lust. He got up at night, went to an old man and told him his thoughts. The old man comforted him, and he returned to his cell strengthened. But the struggle began again in him. Again he went to the old man. And he did this many times. The old man did not reproach him, but spoke to him of what might help him, saying to him, 'Do not give way, but rather come back here and tell me every time the demon wars against you.'

And the brother treated the demon with contempt and he disappeared when he was despised. For, truly, nothing annoys the demon of lust like revealing his works, and nothing pleases him like concealing one's thoughts.

These sayings also offer help to us in dealing with other intense temptations and besetting or habitual sins.

September 22

PSALM 19:12–13   ISAIAH 61:1–3   ROMANS 7:21–25A

A brother overcome by lust went to see a great old man and begged him for help, saying, 'Be so good as to pray for me, for I am overcome by lust.' And the old man prayed to God for him.

A second time he went to the old man and said the same thing, and once more the old man did not omit to plead with God for him, saying, 'Lord, reveal to me the way this brother lives and how this intervention of the devil comes about, for I have already prayed to You, yet he has not found peace.'

Then God revealed this to him about the brother: he saw him sitting with the spirit of lust beside him and an angel, sent to his aid, was standing beside him and becoming angry with him because he did not fall down before God, but instead, taking pleasure in his thoughts, yielded his spirit completely to the action of the devil. So the old man knew that the cause of the trouble was the brother himself, and he told him, 'It is you who are consenting to your thoughts.'

Then he taught him how to resist thoughts, and the brother, restored by the old man's prayer and teaching, found rest.

An old man said, 'What condemns us is not that the thoughts enter into us, but that we use them badly: indeed, through our thoughts we can be shipwrecked, yet through our thoughts we can be found worthy to wear a crown.'

September 23 *Adamnan*

PSALM 112:1 PROVERBS 14:16, 26 JAMES 3:13–18

A brother asked an old man, 'How does the fear of God come into the soul?'

And the old man said, 'If a man has humility and poverty and if he does not judge anyone, the fear of God comes to him.'

September 24

PSALM 30:1–12 LAMENTATIONS 3:26 LUKE 6:20–23

Abba Pastor said, 'Any trial whatever that comes to you can be conquered by silence.'

Amma Syncletica said, 'There is labour and great struggle for unruly souls who are converted to God, but after that comes inexpressible joy. A man who wants to light a fire first is plagued by smoke, and the smoke drives him to tears; yet finally he gets the fire that he wants. So also we ought to light the divine fire in ourselves with labour and with tears.'

September 25 *Cadoc*

PSALM 5:4–8   LEVITICUS 19:18   PHILIPPIANS 2:3–4

An old man said, 'Every time a thought of superiority or vanity moves you, examine yourself to see if you have kept all the commandments; if you love your enemies and are grieved at their sins; if you consider yourself as an unprofitable servant and the greatest sinner of all. Even then, do not pretend to great ideas as though you were perfectly right, for this thought unravels and destroys all that is good.'

September 26

PSALM 119:33–35   DEUTERONOMY 11:13–15
HEBREWS 10:19–23

John of Thebes said, 'The monk must be before all else humble. This is the first commandment of the Lord, who said: Blessed are the poor of spirit, for theirs is the kingdom of heaven.'

Abba Hyperichius said, 'What a monk has to do is obey, and if he does this, then what he asks in prayer will be granted, and he will stand with confidence before the crucified Christ: for thus the Lord Himself came to His cross, being made obedient unto death.'

September 27

PSALM 17:15   ISAIAH 30:15–18   EPHESIANS 1:17–19A

It was said that there were three friends who were unafraid of hard work. The first chose to reconcile those who were fighting each other, because it is said, *Blessed are the peacemakers*. The second chose to visit the sick. The third went to live in prayer and stillness in the desert.

Now in spite of all his labours, the first could not make peace in every quarrel; and in his sorrow he went to the one who was serving the sick, and he found him also disheartened, for he could not fulfil that commandment either. So they went together to see the one who was living in the stillness of prayer. They told him their difficulties and begged him to tell them what to do.

After a short silence, he poured some water into a bowl and said to them, 'Look at the water,' and it was disturbed. After a little while he said to them again, 'Look how still the water is now,' and as they looked into the water, they saw their own faces reflected in it as in a mirror.

Then he said to them, 'It is the same for those who live among people: disturbances prevent them from seeing their own faults. But when someone is still, especially in the desert, then he sees his failings.'

September 28

PSALM 119:1–3   PROVERBS 4:20–23; 27:19   LUKE 6:43–45

An old man said, 'If one is not vigilant about the inner life it is not possible to guard the outward life.'

September 29 *Michael and all angels*

PSALM 119:4–8   PROVERBS 4:24–27   ROMANS 12:1–2

> An old man said, 'The reason why we do not make progress
> is that we do not have the measure of ourselves, and we do
> not persevere in the work we undertake, and we want to
> acquire virtue without labour.'

September 30

PSALM 119:9–16   PROVERBS 4:13; 5:1–2
I THESSALONIANS 5:19–24

> An old man said, 'The prophets wrote books, then came our
> Fathers who put them into practice. Those who came after
> them learnt them by heart. Then came the present genera-
> tion, who have written them out and placed them in seats by
> the window, but without using them.'

Lord, please keep me from accumulating books, ideas and information about You in my head without absorbing Scripture, truth
and the knowledge of You into my heart.

Teach me not just to know more about You, but to desire to
know You more.

October

WALKING ON WATER

The readings this month are all taken from *Walking on Water: Reflections on Faith and Art* by Madeleine L'Engle.

October 1

PSALM 119:130   I KINGS 19:11–16   LUKE 15:17–18

When I am constantly running there is no time for being. When there is no time for being there is no time for listening.

October 2

PSALM 40:8   I KINGS 19:19–21   JOHN 14:10–12

God, through the angel Gabriel, called on Mary to do what, in the world's eyes, is impossible, and instead of saying 'I can't,' she replied immediately, 'Be it unto me according to Thy Word.'

God is always calling on us to do the impossible. It helps me to remember that anything Jesus did during His life here on earth is something we should be able to do, too.

Sometimes, after swimming, I will sit on a sun-warmed rock to dry, and think of Peter walking across the water to meet Jesus. As long as he didn't remember that we human beings have forgotten how to walk on water, he was able to do it.

If Jesus of Nazareth was God become truly man for us, as I believe He was, then we should be able to walk on water, to heal the sick, even to accept the Father's answer to our prayers when it is not the answer we hope for, when it is 'No'. Jesus begged in anguish that He be spared the bitter cup, and then humbly added 'but not as I will, Father: as You will'.

October 3 *Thérèse of Lisieux*

PSALM 119:1–2   2 KINGS 2:1–10   LUKE 1:35–38

How could one young, untried girl contain within her womb the power which created galaxies? How could that power be found in the helplessness of an infant?

What would have happened to Mary (and to the rest of us) if she had said 'No' to the angel? She was free to do so. But she said 'Yes'.

Mary did not always understand. But one does not have to understand to be obedient. Instead of understanding – that intellectual understanding which we are all so fond of – there is a feeling of rightness, of knowing, knowing things which we are not yet able to understand.

October 4 *Francis of Assisi*

PSALM 123:2   2 KINGS 2:11–18   MATTHEW 20:25–27

Servant is an unpopular word, a word we have derided by denigrating servants and service. To serve should be a privilege, and it is to our shame that we tend to think of it as a burden, something to do if you're not fit for anything better or higher.

October 5

PSALM 115:16   2 KINGS 2:19–25   ROMANS 8:18–22

Atheism is a peculiar state of mind: you cannot deny the existence of that which does not exist. I cannot say, 'That chair is not there,' if there is no chair there to say it about.

Many atheists deny God because they care so passion-ately about a caring and personal God; and the world around them is inconsistent with a God of love, they feel, and so they say, 'There is no God.'

The problem of pain, of war and the horror of war, of poverty and disease is always confronting us. But a god who allows no pain, no grief, also allows no choice.

We human beings have been given the terrible gift of free will, and this ability to make choices, to help write our own story, is what makes us human, even when we make the wrong choices, abusing our freedom and the freedom of others. The weary and war-torn world around us bears wit-ness to the wrongness of many of our choices.

October 6

PSALM 40:7–10   2 KINGS 3:9–20   LUKE 9:51

Jesus, too, had to make choices, and in the eyes of the world some of His choices were not only contrary to acceptable behaviour, but were foolish in the extreme. He bucked authority by healing on the Sabbath; when He turned His steps towards Jerusalem He was making a choice which led Him to Calvary.

It is the ability to choose which makes us human.

October 7

PSALM 149:4   2 KINGS 4:1–7   MARK 12:41–44

Often we forget that God has a special gift for each one of us, because we tend to weigh and measure such gifts with the coin of the world's market place. The widow's mite was worth more than all the rich men's gold because it represented the focus of her life. Her poverty was rich because all she had belonged to the living Lord.

October 8

PSALM 119:165   2 KINGS 4:8–17   I CORINTHIANS 13:4–7

We have to be braver than we think we can be, because God is constantly calling us to be more than we are, to see through plastic sham to living, breathing reality, and to break down our defences of self-protection in order to be free to receive and give love.

With God, even a rich man can enter the narrow gate to heaven. Earthbound as we are, even we can walk on water.

Paul certainly wasn't qualified to talk about love. Paul who had persecuted as many Christians as ruthlessly as possible; and yet his poem on love in 1 Corinthians has shattering power. It is not a vague, genial sense of well-being that it offers us, but a particular, painful, birth-giving love.

October 9

PSALM 139:5–6   I KINGS 8:27   I JOHN 3:24

Back somewhere around the eleventh century, Hildevert of Lavardin wrote:

God is over all things,
under all things,
outside all,
within, but not enclosed,
without, but not excluded,
above, but not raised up,
below, but not depressed,

wholly above, presiding,
wholly without, embracing,
wholly within, filling.

October 10 *Paulinus*

PSALM 86:1   2 KINGS 4:36–41   MATTHEW 24:45–46

An old clockmaker and repairer lived in a small village.
When anything was wrong with any of the clocks or
watches in the village, he was able to fix them, to get them
working properly again. When he died, leaving no children
and no apprentice, there was no one left in the village who
could fix clocks. Soon various clocks and watches began to
break down. Those which continued to run lost or gained
time, so they were of little use. A clock might strike midnight at three in the afternoon. So many of the villagers
abandoned their timepieces.

One day a renowned clockmaker and repairer came
through the village, and the people crowded around him
and begged him to fix their broken clocks and watches. He
spent many hours looking at the faulty timepieces, and at
last he announced that he could repair only those whose
owners had kept them wound, because they were the only
ones which would be able to remember how to keep time.

So we must daily keep things wound: that is, we must
pray when prayer seems dry as dust; we must continue
when we are physically tired, when our hearts are heavy,
when our bodies are in pain.

We may not be able to make our 'clock' run correctly,
but at least we can keep it wound, so that it will not forget.

October 11

PSALM 86:2   2 KINGS 4:42–44   MATTHEW 6:10

Canon Tallis says his secretary does not understand that when he is thinking, he is working: she thinks he is wasting time. But thinking time is not wasted time. There are some obvious time-wasters, such as licentious living, drunkenness, adultery, all the things Paul warns us about. A more subtle time-waster is being bored. Jesus was never bored. If we allow our 'high creativity' to remain alive, we will never be bored. We can pray, standing in line at the supermarket. Or we can be lost in awe at all the people around us, their lives full of glory and tragedy, and suddenly we will have the beginnings of a painting, a story, a song.

October 12 *Wilfrid*

PSALM 86:3   2 KINGS 5:1–8   COLOSSIANS 3:17

Not long ago a college senior asked if she could talk to me about being a Christian writer. If she wanted to write Christian fiction, how did she go about it?

I told her that if she is truly and deeply a Christian, what she writes about is going to be Christian, whether she mentions Jesus or not. And if she is not, in the most profound sense, Christian, then what she writes is not going to be Christian, no matter how many times she invokes the name of the Lord.

October 13

PSALM 86:4   2 KINGS 5:9–12   JOHN 19:7

Each time an unexpected discovery is made in the world of knowledge, it shakes the religious establishment of the day. Now, we are often taught that it is unfaithful to question traditional religious beliefs, but I believe we must question them continually – not God, not Christ, who are at the centre of our lives as believers and creators – but what human beings say about God and about Christ; otherwise, like those of the church establishment of Galileo's day, we truly become God's frozen people. Galileo's discoveries did nothing to change the nature of God; they threatened only man's rigid ideas of the nature of God. We must constantly be open to new revelation, which is another way of hearing God, with loving obedience.

We must be kept from frozenness, from smugness, from thinking that the truth is in us, rather than in God, in Christ our Lord. We are closer to God in our doubts than in our certainties: it is all right to be like a small child who constantly asks: Why? Why? Why?

October 14

PSALM 86:5   2 KINGS 5:13–19A   JAMES 4:8A

To pray is to listen also, to move through my own chattering to God, to that place where I can be silent and listen to what God might have to say. But, if I pray only when I feel like it, God may not choose to speak. The greatest moments of prayer come in the midst of fumbling and faltering prayer, rather than in the odd moment when one decides to try to turn to God.

October 15 *Teresa of Avila*

PSALM 86:6   2 KINGS 5:19B–27   JOHN 19:7

In an interview in a well-known Christian magazine, I
explained earnestly that we are limited by our points of
view. 'I have a point of view,' I told the interviewer, 'you
have a point of view. But *God* has *view*.' When the article
appeared, some over-diligent copy editor had changed it to,
'I have a point of view. You have a point of view. God has a
point of view.'

I wrote back in a white heat. 'This is a theological error.
Please correct it. The *point* is…'

October 16 *Gall*

PSALM 86:7   2 KINGS 6:1–7   LUKE 23:26

In our daily living the actions we choose, from within our
own skins, as the best possible under the circumstances,
may well turn out to have been the wrong ones. Something
we regret at the time as abysmally stupid may well end up
being the one thing needed under the circumstances. We are
trapped in unknowing.

Nothing is certain. I sat writing on my first novel, quite
bogged down, and in annoyance at my own lack of creativity got up and walked across the room. As I reached the
window, the heavily-moulded plaster ceiling crashed down
where I had just been sitting.

My husband came home on the subway train just before
the one that had the accident; someone else's husband
didn't.

October 17

PSALM 86:8   2 KINGS 6:8–22   MATTHEW 27:3–8

Far too often in this confused world we are faced with choices, *all* of which are wrong, and the only thing we can do, in fear and trembling, is to choose the least wrong, without pretending to ourselves that it is right.

It is a criterion of love. In moments of decision, we are to try to make what seems to be the most loving, the most creative, decision. We are not to play safe, to draw back out of fear. Love may well lead us into danger. It may lead us to die for our friend. In a day when we are taught to look for easy solutions, it is not always easy to hold on to that most difficult one of all, love.

October 18

PSALM 86:9   2 KINGS 6:23–7:2   MATTHEW 5:17–18

During a summer season at Wheaton, one of the students asked, 'Do you think there are any absolutes?'

I thought for a second and then said, off the top of my head, 'Yes, I think the ten commandments are absolutes.' Later, as I set them against the great works of literature, they seemed to hold fast. When we break one of the commandments, we are doing something we would not want children to see. We are being destructive, rather than creative. We are taking things into our own hands and playing God. Whenever the first commandment is broken, more breakage follows.

October 19

PSALM 86:10   2 KINGS 7:3–20   2 CORINTHIANS 3:12–18

A cloud covered Jesus and Moses and Elijah, that extraordinary cloud which signals God With Us. As Gregory of Nyssa points out, when Moses first talked with God, he talked in the light, but as he grew in spiritual stature he talked with God in the darkness. But what darkness! When Moses came down from the mountain his face shone with such brilliance that the people could not bear to look at him, and after that whenever he went into the darkness of the cloud to talk with God, he had to cover his face when he returned, so that the brilliance of his countenance would not blind the people.

October 20

PSALM 86:11   2 KINGS 8:1–3   MARK 12:30

In prayer, these two parts of ourselves, the mind and the heart, the intellect and the intuition, the conscious and subconscious mind, stop fighting each other and collaborate. Theophan the Recluse advised those who came to him for counsel to 'pray with the mind in the heart,' and surely this is how the artist works. When the mind and the heart work together, they know each other as two people who love each other know; and as the love of two people is a gift, a totally unmerited, incomprehensible gift, so is the union of mind and heart. David cried out to God, 'Unite my heart to fear Thy Name.' It is my prayer, too.

October 21 *Tuda*

PSALM 86:12   2 KINGS 8:4–6   EPHESIANS 5:33–6:3

I was at the annual meeting of a state library association ... when the children were in the process of leaving the nest, and one of the librarians asked me, 'What do you think you and Hugh have done which was best for your children?'

I answered immediately and without thinking, 'We love each other.'

October 22

PSALM 86:13   2 KINGS 8:7–15   JAMES 1:22–25

No matter where I am, at home, abroad, I begin the day with morning prayer, including the Psalms for the day, so that at the end of the month I have gone through the book of Psalms. I also read from both the Old and New Testaments. And there is almost always something in the Psalms or the other Scripture which I need to hear for that day, something I may have read hundreds of times before, but which suddenly springs out at me with new meaning.

I end the day, in the same way, with evening prayer, and this gives the day a structure.

October 23

PSALM 86:14   2 KINGS 9:1–13   EPHESIANS 5:18B

And then there is time in which to be, simply to be, that time in which God quietly tells us who we are and who He wants us to be. It is then that God can take our emptiness and fill it up with what He wants, and drain away the business with which we inevitably get involved in the dailiness of human living.

October 24

PSALM 86:15   2 KINGS 13:14–17   MATTHEW 19:14

Vulnerability is something we instinctively reject because we are taught from kindergarten on that we must protect ourselves, control our behaviour and our lives. But, in becoming man for us, Christ made Himself totally vulnerable for us in Jesus of Nazareth, and it is not possible to be a Christian while refusing to be vulnerable.

We are, ourselves, as little children, and therefore we are vulnerable. We might paraphrase Descartes to read, 'I hurt, therefore I am.'

October 25

PSALM 86:16   2 KINGS 13:18–19   MATTHEW 5:44–45

Because of the great affirmation of the incarnation, we may not give in to despair. Nor superstition.

Being a Christian, being saved, does not mean that nothing bad is ever going to happen. Terrible things happen to Christians as well as to Hindus and Buddhists and hedonists and atheists. To human beings. When the phone rings at an unexpected hour my heart lurches. I love, therefore I am vulnerable.

When we were children, we used to think that when we were grown up we would no longer be vulnerable. But to grow up is to accept vulnerability.

October 26 Cedd Eata

PSALM 86:17   2 KINGS 13:20–21   JOHN 18:10–11

Homo Sapiens. Man who knows. Or rather, *man who is conscious* would be more accurate. Man who is conscious that he does not know. Has there been a loss of knowing since Adam and Eve, rather than a gaining? Despite all our technology there is far more that we do not know than that we know, and the most terrible defect is our inability to tell right from wrong, to do horrible things for all the right reasons and then to blunder inadvertently into doing something which turns out to be good. We try to make the loving, the creative decision, but we cannot *know* whether or not we are right.

Alleluia! We don't have to be right! We do have to love, to be vulnerable, to accept joy and pain, and grow through them.

October 27

PSALM 93:1   RUTH 1:1–18   JOHN 21:2–3

Was it predetermined that Milton go blind in order to write *Paradise Lost*? That Beethoven go deaf to write the Ninth Symphony? That these artists grew through affliction is undeniable, but that this affliction was planned? No! Everything in me rebels. I cannot live in a world where everything is predetermined, an ant world in which there is no element of choice. I do believe that we all have a share in the writing of our own story. We do make a decision at the crossroads. Milton could have retreated into passive blindness and self-pity instead of trying the patience of his three dutiful daughters and any visiting friend by insisting that they write down what he dictated. Beethoven could have remained in the gloom of silence instead of forging the glorious sounds which he could never hear except in his artist's imagination. Sometimes the very impetus of overcoming obstacles results in a surge of creativity. It is in our responses that we are given the gift of helping God write our story.

October 28

PSALM 93:2   RUTH 2:8–13   I PETER 1:22–25

In contemplative prayer the saint (who knows himself to be a sinner, for none of us is whole, healed and holy twenty-four hours a day) turns inwards in what is called 'the prayer of heart,' not to find self, but to lose self in order to be found.

We have been afraid of this kind of prayer, we of the twentieth-century Judaeo-Christian tradition. It is not talked about in many temples or churches. And so those intuitively seeking it have been forced to look for it elsewhere.

Why have we been afraid of it? Because it is death, and no matter how loudly we protest, we are afraid of death.

October 29

PSALM 93:3   RUTH 3:1–11   JOHN 3:1–12

Many young people have asked me about Hindu or Buddhist or Sufi methods of meditation, and are astounded, and sometimes disbelieving, when I tell them that we have such a Way within our own tradition.

The techniques of contemplation are similar in all traditions, just as a pianist, no matter what kind of music he is going to play, must do his finger exercises. But ultimately the aim is different. For the easterner the goal is *nirvana*, which means 'where there is no wind,' and for us the wind of the Spirit is vital, even when it blows harshly. We do not move from meditation into contemplation, into self-annihilation, into death, in order to be freed from the intolerable wheel of life. No. We move – are moved – into death in order to be discovered, to be loved into truer life by our Maker. To die to self in the prayer of contemplation is to move to a meeting of lovers.

October 30

PSALM 93:4 RUTH 3:13–4:6 MATTHEW 14:22–31

When Jesus called Peter to come to him across the water, Peter for one brief, glorious moment, remembered how, and strode with ease across the lake. This is how we are meant to be, and then we forget, and we sink. But if we cry out for help (as Peter did) we will be pulled out of the water, we won't drown. And if we listen, we will hear; and if we look, we will see.

The impossible still happens to us; sometimes when we are so tired that inadvertently we let down all the barriers we have built up. We lose our adult scepticism and become once again children who can walk.

October 31 All Hallows Eve Begu

PSALM 93:5 RUTH 4:7–17 MATTHEW 14:26

Last spring I was giving a series of talks at the Cathedral of St Peter in St Petersburg, Florida, and was staying with parishioners who had a house right by the water. I was unusually tired; into an already overcrowded schedule I'd had to interject trips to England and to Jerusalem, and in Jerusalem I'd fallen and bashed my ribs ('You've *wrinkled* your ribs,' the doctor reading the x-rays told me), and I was strapped up and in considerable pain. One afternoon I had a couple of hours to myself, and so I limped to the seawall and stretched out and closed my eyes and tried to let go all my aches and pains and tiredness, to let go and simply be. And while I was lying there, eased by the cool breezes, the warm sun, bursts of bird song, I heard feet coming towards me, a familiar sound: the feet of Jesus coming towards me.

And then another noise broke in, and I was back in an aching body. But I had heard. For a moment in that hearing I was freed from the dirty devices of this world. I was more than I am. I was healed.

It is one of those impossibilities I believe in; and in believing, my own feet touch the surface of the lake, and I go to meet Him, like Peter walking on water.

November

PROTECTIVE CLOTHING

These readings provide us with prayers suitable for memorizing and repeating aloud. Such prayers prepare us for the real world – its temptations and lies – helping us to understand from the heart about guilt and attack, love, forgiveness and protection. It is part of Celtic tradition to put on Christ even as we dress ourselves. Maybe one or more of these prayers will suit you well, and be worn as part of your own 'protective clothing'.

Many of the readings are drawn from Father Gilbert Shaw's *A Pilgrim's Book of Prayers*.

November 1 All Saints

PSALM 118:22   PROVERBS 27:6A   JOHN 19:37

O heart of Jesus, be my peace!
Your wounded side my home,
Your broken feet my following.

Gilbert Shaw

November 2

PSALM 138:1–2   I CHRONICLES 29:18   ACTS 17:24–28

O God,
it is enough for me to say
again and yet again
this word descriptive
of Yourself:
the Indescribable
in whom we live
and move

and have our being:
God, my God, my all,
my life, my God.

Gilbert Shaw

November 3

PSALM 118:24   I CHRONICLES 29:11-14   COLOSSIANS 1:19-20

O God of mercy, God of grace,
teach me to hold myself so still,
within the inmost centre of my soul,
that I may know all things are Yours
and none are mine unless You give to me
that I and they may bless Your Name.

Gilbert Shaw

November 4

PSALM 51:10, 12   DEUTERONOMY 10:20-21   LUKE 23:42

Jesus,
may I by repetition of Your Name
always remember You
with my whole thinking,
with desire and affection,
with all my imagination,
with all my memory,
understanding, reason and attention.

Gilbert Shaw

November 5

PSALM 51:15   DEUTERONOMY 11:13–17   JOHN 12:3

> Jesus,
> may I by repetition of Your Name
> be drawn to You so close
> in worshipping response,
> to hold You still,
> that I may know
> the living quiet of Your love,
> the love that passes understanding.

Gilbert Shaw

November 6 *Illtyd*

PSALM 51:15   SONG OF SONGS 5:2–8; 5:16–6:3   JOHN 20:16

> Jesus, Beloved,
> You are mine
> and I am Yours.
> You stand at the lattice;
> I sought You and You found me;
> I lost You, and I seek You
> in the repetition of Your Name.
>
> Jesus, Beloved,
> I am Yours
> and You are mine.
> I lost You, and am found by You
> in the repetition of Your Name.
>
> You stand at the door;
> my heart is moved in quick response
> by repetition of Your Name.

Gilbert Shaw

November 7 *Willibrord*

PSALM 136:1–3, 10–14   EXODUS 3:4, 7, 13
REVELATION 12:7–11

Blood shed for many,
blood life-giving stream,
blood shed for remission of sins,
blood encompassing all life,
blood destroying death,
blood overcoming him who
had the power of death,
blood by which Michael
was victorious,
blood liberating all from
Satan's power:
I praise the wounds
and the blood of the Lamb.

Gilbert Shaw/Basilea Schlinck

November 8

PSALM 136:12   EXODUS 24:7–8   REVELATION 12:11

Blood of Jesus
sustaining the soul in darkness,
refreshing the soul in light,
source of the victories of the saints:

I praise the wounds
and the blood of the Lamb.

Gilbert Shaw/Basilea Schlinck

November 9

PSALM 136:1–3, 23–24, 26   GENESIS 4:10   HEBREWS 10:19–25

> Blood of the Lamb slain
> from the foundation of the world,
> the same, yesterday, today,
> and forever,
> whom the angels, dominations,
> and powers praise and fear,
> whom the heavens, cherubim,
> and seraphim exalt,
> whom Your people acclaim
> with ceaseless adoration:
>
> blood of the Lamb
> that pleads for sinners
> in the heavenly places,
> one sacrifice, complete.
>
> Lord, by Your blood we pray:
> unite Your people on earth
> and make us one.

Gilbert Shaw

November 10

PSALM 148:8   HABAKKUK 3:2–19   EPHESIANS 6:12–13

In using the rune of Patrick at Tara, you should change the beginning to name the place or situation you are in as you pray it.

> At *(Tara)* today in this fateful hour,
> I place all Heaven with its power,
> and the sun with its brightness,

and the snow with its whiteness,
and fire with all the strength it hath,
and lightning with its rapid wrath,
and the winds with their swiftness along their path,
and the sea with its deepness,
and the earth with its starkness:
all these I place,
by God's almighty help and grace,
between myself and the powers of darkness.

November 11 *Martin of Tours*

PSALM 125:2   ISAIAH 54:2   LUKE 2:9–10

The 'caim' is traditional Celtic prayer with which God, the
saints and angels were called in to the aid of those in need.
An imaginary circle is made by anyone in fear, danger or
distress by stretching out the right hand with the forefinger
extended and turning sun-wise, as though on a pivot, so that
the circle enclosed and accompanied the man or woman as
they walked, and safeguarded them from all evil, within or
without.

Esther de Waal, Celtic Vision

Circle me, O God:
keep hope within, despair without;
keep peace within, keep turmoil out,
O my loving God.

Circle me, O God:
keep love within, keep hatred out;
keep calm within, and storms without,
O my loving God.

Circle me, O God:
keep strength within; keep weakness out;
keep light within and darkness out,
O my loving God.

When my heart is hard,
keep Your light in front of me.
When my tongue is sharp,
keep Your light in front of me;
when my eyes are far away from You;
when I need someone:
Circle in the dark,
keep Your light in front of me.

When the winds are howl,
keep Your light in front of me.
When the pain is now,
keep Your light in front of me;
when the moon is lost behind the clouds:
Circle in the dark,
keep Your light in front of me.
I need someone.

Circle me, O God!

> *From a prayer by David Adam in* The Edge of Glory,
> *and a song by Coleman and Bartle of L'Arche Community*
> *in Australia*

November 12

PSALM 147:14–15   I KINGS 8:10–11   ACTS 4:30–31

You, Lord, are in this place –
Your presence fills it.
Your presence is peace.

You, Lord, are in my life –
Your presence fills it.
Your presence is peace.

You, Lord, are in my heart –
Your presence fills it.
Your presence is peace.

David Adam

November 13

PSALM 5:11–12   EXODUS 18:1–11   EPHESIANS 6:17–19

God be in my head,
and in my understanding;
God be in mine eyes,
and in my looking;
God be in my mouth,
and in my speaking;
God be in my heart,
and in my thinking;
God be at mine end,
and at my departing.

From a Sarum primer

November 14

PSALM 86:10–11   JOSHUA 14:6–14; 15:13–16   MATTHEW 5:19

A student is not above his teacher, nor a servant above his
master. It is enough for the student to be like his teacher,
and the servant like his master.

Matthew 10:24–25a

O Lord, I pray that in You
I'll break ground both fresh and new.
As a student let me stand,
break the hardness of the land
with Your forgiving Father-hand.

From 'Student Song' by Paul Stamper

November 15

PSALM 3:2–6, 8   JOSHUA 9:3–27   MATTHEW 5:9

They
drew a circle
and
counted me out;

but God and I had
a will to win!
We
drew a circle
and
counted them
in!

Arthur Burt, Pebbles to Slay Goliath

November 16   *Celtic Advent begins*

PSALM 16:5–7   ISAIAH 30:15–18   MATTHEW 6:6

Most of us crave solitude. As our lives grow more pressured, as we grow more tired, we fantasize about solitude.
We make solitude yet another activity, something we will
do. We attempt to take solitude like taking a shower. It
is understood as something we stand under, endure, get
washed by – and then return to normal life.

Solitude, however, is a form of awareness. It is a way of being present and perceptive within all of life. It is having a dimension of reflectiveness in our ordinary lives that brings with it a sense of gratitude, appreciation, peacefulness, enjoyment and prayer. It is the sense within ordinary life that ordinary life is precious, sacred and enough.

Ronald Rolheiser, Forgotten among the Lilies

November 17   *Hild*

PSALM 119:35   I KINGS 19:19–21   LUKE 8:35

Oh, with a gesture light and free,
Lord, I would give my life to Thee –
not solemnly –
not grudgingly!

No! I would take my life and fling
it at Thy feet and sing – and sing –
so I might bring
Thee this small thing!

Mary Dixon Thayer, Songs before the Blessed Sacrament

November 18

PSALM 119:58   ISAIAH 30:15   LUKE 22:61A

Father,
I ask You to take from me now all that harasses and annoys,
all that has laid upon my heart burdens of anxiety and care.
I thank You for the stillness of this time of prayer –
this oasis in my busy day when I can relax before You,
lay my burdens down,
and hand over to You all my anxieties.

At this moment,

I open my heart to receive Your blessing,
knowing that in Your presence:

the furrows are being smoothed from my brow,
the lines from my face,
the load from my heart,
the doubts from my mind,
the fears from my soul;
that I am at peace.

The Prayers of Peter Marshall

November 19

PSALM 78:1–2   I SAMUEL 3:1, 8–10   JOHN 3:8–12

In the silence of the stars,
in the quiet of the hills,
in the heaving of the sea,
speak, Lord.

In the stillness of this room,
in the calming of my mind
in the longing of my heart,
speak, Lord.

In the voice of a friend,
in the chatter of a child,
in the words of a stranger,
speak, Lord.

In the opening of a book,
in the looking at a film,
in the listening to music,
speak, Lord,
for Your servant listens.

David Adam, Borderlands

November 20

PSALM 90:14   EXODUS 15:11   JOHN 12:2–3

I am giving Thee worship with my whole life, every hour;
I am giving Thee assent with my whole power,
with my fill of tongue's utterance I am giving Thee praise;
I am giving Thee honour with my whole lays.

I am giving Thee loving with my devotion's whole art;
I am giving kneeling with my whole desire;
I am giving Thee liking with my whole beating of heart;
I am giving affection with my sense-fire;
I am giving mine existing with my mind and its whole.

O God of all gods, I am giving my soul.

Mary Gillies of Morar,
from Martin Reith's God in our Midst

November 21

PSALM 61:1–3   I SAMUEL 10:17   LUKE 24:14–15

Jesus, so dear to us,
Jesus, be near to us,
Jesus, give ear to us
each as we pray.
Jesus, whate'er betide,
Jesus, be friend and guide,
Jesus, be by our side
now and for aye.

V. Hill

November 22 C. S. Lewis

PSALM 80:17–19   I SAMUEL 17:38–39   EPHESIANS 6:10–13

So stand ready with truth as a belt;
with righteousness as your breast-plate;
and as your shoes the readiness to announce the good news
   of peace;
at all times carry faith as a shield, for with it you will be
   able to put out all the burning arrows shot by the evil one;
and accept salvation as a helmet;
and the word of God as the sword which the Spirit gives
   you:

Father, we know You want a people who will live by the
red-hot word that proceeds out of the mouth of God. Help
us to live by the proceeding word. Examine our motives,
and cut through our hearts, dividing between soul and
spirit, between all we rely on and our need to rely on You
just now.

Andy Raine, Battle Cry

November 23 *Columbanus*

PSALM 132:9   JOB 29:11–16   2 CORINTHIANS 5:1–8

Be Thou my vision, O Lord of my heart,
naught be all else to me save that Thou art.
Thou my best thought in the day and the night,
waking or sleeping, Thy presence my light.

Be Thou my wisdom, be Thou my true word,
I ever with Thee, and Thou with me, Lord.
Thou my great Father, and I Thy true son,
Thou in me dwelling, and I with Thee one.

Be Thou my breastplate, my sword for the fight,
be Thou my armour, and be Thou my might.
Thou my soul's shelter, and Thou my high tower,
raise Thou me heavenwards, O power of my power.

Riches I heed not, nor man's empty praise,
Thou mine inheritance through all of my days.
Thou and Thou only the first in my heart,
High King of heaven, my treasure Thou art.

O High King of heaven, when battle is done,
grant heaven's joy to me, bright heaven's sun.
Christ of my own heart, whatever befall,
still be Thou my vision, O Ruler of all.

Ancient Irish, translated by Mary Byrne

AT HIS FEET

The following readings are based on old-fashioned hymns inspired by Scripture.

November 24 *Eanfleda*

PSALM 143:1–5   GENESIS 28:10–13, 15–21   JAMES 4:8

Though, like the wanderer,
the sun gone down,
darkness be over me,
my rest a stone,
yet in my dreams I'd be
nearer, my God, to Thee,
nearer to Thee.

There let the way appear
steps up to heaven;
all that Thou sendest me
in mercy given;
angels to beckon me
nearer, my God, to Thee,
nearer to Thee.

Then, with my waking thoughts
bright with Thy praise,
out of my stony griefs
Bethel I'll raise;
so by my woes to be
nearer, my God, to Thee,
nearer to Thee.

Sarah Adams

Times of crisis, of deep pain or joy, or that strange mingling of the two which we sometimes encounter – these are the very times when the traffic between earth and heaven is more evident, the veil between is pierced and God's ever-presence can be rooted firmly in our heart and faith story.

November 25

PSALM 144:9–10   2 SAMUEL 15:21   JOHN 12:26

O Jesus, Thou hast promised,
to all who follow Thee,
that where Thou art in glory
there shall Thy servant be;
and, Jesus, I have promised
to serve Thee to the end;
oh, give me grace to follow
my Master and my Friend.

Oh, let me feel Thee near me:
the world is ever near;
I see the sights that dazzle,
the tempting sounds I hear.
My foes are ever near me,
around me and within;
but, Jesus, draw Thou nearer,
and shield my soul from sin.

J. E. Bode

There is great simplicity in a life that is given.

My will is to do the will of Him who sent me.
I will be with You.
Where You go, there will Your servant be.
My will is less important than Yours.

This is the freedom of simplicity: I want God to know that He can count on me.

November 26

PSALM 145:1   2 CHRONICLES 5:13–14   MATTHEW 3:11

> To make our weak hearts strong and brave,
> send the fire!
> To live a dying world to save,
> send the fire!
> Oh, see us on Your altar lay our lives, our all,
> this very day;
> to crown the offering now we pray,
> send the fire!

William Booth

A good look in the mirror for some can reveal a lifeless face which is not really ours, and dull eyes, our own, but hidden deeply beneath a lying glass.

Our eyes and face, leathery, ossified, blank, distant, devoid of innocence and virginity; somewhere (so gradually it happens) our fire went out! What's to be done? My suggestion is that we take a good long look at ourselves in a mirror. Study the eyes, stare long and hard. Let what we see frighten us enough to move us towards the road of unlearning and 're-virginization'. Look in a mirror, look at your face until some of the self-preoccupation, the cynicism, the pseudo-sophistication, and the unchastity and adultness drops away. Stare into your eyes until the lying glass breaks and you see there again the little boy or girl who once inhabited that space. In that, wonder will be born.

Our eyes seldom grow tired, though they frequently get buried. It is the latter which causes the blank passionless stare. Bodies tire, but eyes are linked to spirits...

The Christian's eyes are staring with frantic intenseness outwards.

Ronald Rolheiser, Forgotten among the Lilies

November 27

PSALM 145:5–7   2 KINGS 4:1–7   LUKE 5:4

He will fill your hearts today to overflowing,
as the Lord commanded you,
'Bring your vessels not a few.'
He will fill your hearts today to overflowing
with His Holy Ghost and power.

Mrs C. H. Morris

Miracles are coming towards you or passing you by every day. The difference is that some people have their arms open to welcome them, and others are looking the other way while the miracles pass over their shoulder.

Oral Roberts

November 28

PSALM 145:8–9   JOB 23:10   LUKE 12:32

Wherever He may guide me,
no want shall turn me back;
my Shepherd is beside me,
and nothing shall I lack.
His wisdom ever waketh,
His sight is never dim;
He knows the way He taketh,
and I will walk with Him.

Anna L. Waring

Each of us is responsible for developing our own relationship with the true Shepherd. He calls us by name, and we know His voice well enough not to confuse it with the voice of a stranger. When the deceiver comes we say with confidence, 'My Shepherd would never say that.' We do not follow the deceiver's voice, but continue gazing into the pastures already allotted to us.

November 29

PSALM 145:20–21   ZECHARIAH 13:1   REVELATION 7:9–10

There is a fountain filled with blood,
drawn from Immanuel's veins,
and sinners, plunged beneath that flood,
lose all their guilty stains.

I do believe, I will believe,
that Jesus died for me!
that on the cross He shed His blood
from sin to set me free.

E'er since by faith I saw the stream
Thy flowing wounds supply,
redeeming love has been my theme,
and shall be till I die.

William Cowper

It is all a little gruesome, this talk about blood, but life can depend upon the shedding of blood. Sin means death, but life is in the blood.

This biblical obsession with blood may seem Gothic, or even as absurd as a Hammer horror movie, but when evil threatens it is the power of the cross and blood spilt from it that is our protection and victory – we must never be ashamed of that. Jesus was not squeamish. He did not say, 'Oh, please don't crucify Me; I can't stand the sight of blood!'

November 30

PSALM 146:9–10   ISAIAH 42:11   ACTS 4:32

Blest be the tie that binds
our hearts in Christian love;
the fellowship of kindred minds
is like to that above.

We share our mutual woes,
our mutual burdens bear;
and often for each other flows
the sympathizing tear.

When we asunder part,
it gives us inward pain;
but we shall still be joined in heart,
and hope to meet again.

John Fawcett

Be in the heart of each to whom I speak,
in the mouth of each who speaks unto me.

St Patrick's Breastplate

Then friends are friends for ever if the Lord's the Lord of
them, and a lifetime's not too long to live as friends.

Michael Smith

December

JESSE TREE

The title of this month's readings is the name which was given to depictions in stained glass of the characters who are part of Jesus' family tree, from Jesse through David to Joseph and Mary.

In many homes and churches it has become an Advent custom to have a small tree branch as a Jesse tree, which is stripped, painted gold, white or silver, and then hung with pictures or ornaments representing the people, prophecies and stories which anticipated the coming of Christ. Some churches have a special Jesse tree service, at which the ornaments are added one at a time, and the stories recalled one by one. At home it is probably more beneficial to read the accompanying scriptures day by day, and add the pictures or ornaments so that, rather like the pictures in an Advent calendar, more and more appear as Christmas approaches.

You may wish to prepare your own Jesse tree by choosing a branch which can be suspended from a ceiling or 'planted' in a pot, and copying a double set of the pictures to stick together back to back. Alternatively, you may like to make or collect your own set of pictures or ornaments.

As a family we have come to love and appreciate having the Jesse tree as a focal point during December. We find that it offsets and pre-empts the onset of an increasingly commercial and secularized Christmas. Each day a different ornament is unpacked from the case, and a familiar story revisited. Our favourite is the purple banner of the Lion of Judah, with a beautiful and magnificent face of Aslan gazing goldenly from it. We made a whale with a tiny Jonah suspended by a thread in its open mouth. The manna pot has been known to contain white chocolate buttons… (In our house, the Christmas tree has its place, but it is not the spiritual focus of the festival!) The picture of a perfect, unborn baby which hangs on our Jesse tree has, on closer inspection, a different flesh-coloured image on its reverse – the faces and shoulders of a couple held in each other's embrace, etched within the outline of the foetus.

Some of the figures (produced here for us by Sara Bennett-Steele) and readings remind us of the direct genealogies of Jesus through Noah, Jacob, Judah, Rahab, Ruth, Jesse, David, Solomon and Zerubbabel. Some are rich in prophetic significance and recall the blood of Abel, the forgiving love of Joseph, the resurrection of Jonah, and Isaiah's foretelling of the reign of the Prince of Peace. The remaining days of December continue the story, and mark the feasts of Stephen, the 'holy innocents' slaughtered by Herod, and John the beloved. They remind us of the covenant that Jesus, the promised Messiah, invites us all to enter into with Him.

Whether you create your own Jesse tree this year or not, we hope these readings will provide a focus for prayer and memory, a spur to the imagination, and that the journey through image and Scripture in this month of December will again enkindle a flame of love and wonder as we enjoy the coming of Jesus, the promised One.

December 1 *Charles de Foucauld*

PSALM 78:17   GENESIS 1:2–4   MATTHEW 5:44–45

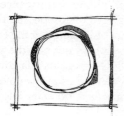

THE SUN
The people of the islands of the Hebrides called the sun
'the eye of the great God'
because God looks on us
in warmth and love,
giving us life and light.
And they would bow the head
in reverence to God.

I bow my head to You, Lord God
who made the sun, and all that lives.
You are the true light –
a light which touches
every person born into the world.

December 2 *Jean Donovan*

PSALM 8:3–9   GENESIS 2:15–17; 3:1–13   REVELATION 22:1–2

THE FRUIT OF THE TREE
'Are you sure that God said, No?
Aren't you grown-up enough to
make your own decisions?
One little taste won't hurt;
besides, you might like it.'

Then suddenly we know
only too well,
and begin to make excuses –
'It's not my fault…'
'I didn't mean it…'
'I couldn't help it…'
'The temptation was too great…'

December 3

PSALM 22:9–11   GENESIS 4:1–11   COLOSSIANS 1:19–20

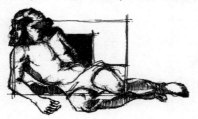

ABEL

'Am I my brother's keeper?' asked Cain.
He should have cared for his younger brother
and looked out for him.
But he didn't.
Instead, he was jealous and killed him.
And the blood of Abel cried out to God
from the ground where he fell.

Jesus watches out for us like an elder brother.
He was killed by jealous men,
and His blood which fell from the cross to the ground
still cries out to the Father,
'Forgive them! They don't know what they are doing.'

And what about me?
Am I my brother's keeper?

December 4

PSALM 105:7   GENESIS 6:13–14   HEBREWS 11:7

NOAH'S ARK

The people thought that Noah was a fool.
He built a wooden boat called an ark,
miles away from the sea.
Noah warned the people that God was angry
with all the evil things they did.
God was sad that they didn't want to love Him
and trust Him
like Noah and his family did.

Then the rain came, just as Noah had said.
Noah could shelter in the ark
just as God had shown him.
When the water covered the land
and reached the ark,
the ark floated on top of the waters.

December 5

PSALM 105:8   GENESIS 22:2, 6–14   ROMANS 8:31–32

THE SON ON THE ALTAR
'Abraham, your son must be killed –
your son, your only son,
the son you love.'
'Oh, God,' said Abraham,
'You don't know what it means
to give your son like that.'
But Abraham gave his son,
the son he loved;
and Isaac's life was spared.

God loved the world so much
that He gave His only Son;
so whoever believes and trusts
in Him will no longer be dying,
but come alive in Jesus.

December 6

PSALM 105:9   GENESIS 24:10–20, 55–59, 62–66
JOHN 4:7, 13–15

THE CAMEL AND THE WATER JAR
Rebekah leaves her home and family
and trusts in God
who is bringing her to a man
she has never met,
but is to love and marry.
'I will go,' she says,
'let nothing hold me back
from the new life
that is waiting for me.'

She journeys into the desert
with a heart that reaches forward
and waits to give itself to love.

December 7 *Diuma*

PSALM 105:10–11   GENESIS 28:10–17   LUKE 2:13–14

THE LADDER
Heaven is not far away
if only our eyes were open
to see how kind God's heart is.
His messengers bring peace,
and tell us that God
wants all that is best for us.
Heaven is not far away,
and surely the Lord is here
where we are.

December 8

PSALM 105:5–6   GENESIS 49:1–2, 9–10   REVELATION 5:1–14

THE LION BANNER
The King is coming!
He is called the Lion,
the Lion of the tribe of Judah;
and all the people
will gather to Him.
He came to us, gave us His life;
He lives again;
and He will come in glory!

December 9

PSALM 105:12–22   GENESIS 37:3–13   LUKE 1:76–77

THE COAT OF MANY COLOURS
Joseph's coat is brightest of all.
Joseph is the chosen one,
honoured more than his brothers.
Joseph is the prophet, the dreamer of dreams;
chosen for honour, chosen for disgrace,
chosen to suffer.
Joseph was true to God and
true to his dreams.
It meant nakedness, shame,
reproach and false accusation.

Do I dare
be a dreamer for God's kingdom?

December 10

PSALM 105:26–27   EXODUS 3:2–5   LUKE 1:34–35

THE BURNING BUSH

When Moses was tending his father-in-law's flocks,
out on the edge of the desert,
suddenly the angel of the Lord appeared to him
as a flame of fire in a bush.
When Moses saw the bush was on fire
and that it didn't burn up,
he went over to investigate.
Then God spoke to him out of the flame:
'Moses! Moses!'
'Who is it?' Moses asked.
'Don't come any closer,' God told him.
'Take off your shoes,
for you are standing on holy ground,
and I am God who speaks to you.'

God, when I know You're really here,
then where I stand is holy ground!

December 11 *Thomas Merton*

PSALM 105:37–39   EXODUS 13:17–22   I CORINTHIANS 10:1–3

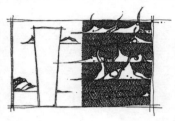

THE PILLAR OF CLOUD AND FIRE
The presence of the Lord
went out before His people
to guide them.
By day, it would be as
a pillar of cloud;
by night, the cloud was on fire.
When the cloud moved
they continued their journey;
when it stopped
they did not dare go further,
but waited for the cloud.

December 12 *Finnian of Clonard*

PSALM 105:40B   EXODUS 16:14–15, 31–33
I CORINTHIANS 10:1–3

MANNA
God had called them to follow Him:
He led them into the desert.
He knew what they needed.
He provided for them.
They said, 'What is this?'
But they didn't go hungry,
and when they tasted
the bread He provided
its taste was sweet.

December 13

PSALM 119:62–64   EXODUS 20:1–9, 12–17; 31:18
ROMANS 13:10

THE TABLETS OF THE LAW
These Laws begin to show us
what God is like,
and how we can begin to be like Him.
Jesus showed us even more clearly:
we should love the Lord our God
with all our heart and strength,
and we should want the best
for everyone we know –
and even for those we have not met.

This is the beginning
of the fulfilling
of the Law which tells us
how to love.

December 14   *John of the Cross*   *Catherine de Hueck Doherty*

PSALM 36:7   EXODUS 25:17–22; 35:30–40
HEBREWS 9:3–5; 10:19–20

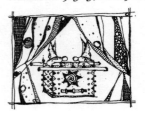

THE ARK OF THE COVENANT
God speaks to us in pictures:
smoke and glory; angels' wings;
light eternal; holy, radiant light
in the centre of all things,
the hidden place behind the veil.

Can God be held, contained
in a box of gold and wood?
Look! God makes His home
here among the people:
the hidden focus of our life.

December 15

PSALM 98:2   JOSHUA 2:1–21; 6:20–25   HEBREWS 11:31

THE SCARLET CORD
Rahab was told by the spies
to hang a scarlet thread
in the window of her house.
Just as the death-angel passed over
the houses of the Israelites
when blood was on the door,
so she would be saved
when the walls came down.
These two men had understood
the importance of the blood.

The scarlet thread stretches
through all of Scripture
and through all time,
saying: Sin means death,
but life is in the blood.

The blood of Jesus touches me;
I live, and I am free.

December 16

PSALM 98:3   RUTH 2:2–9, 14–19; 3:7–9; 4:13–17
MATTHEW 9:36–38

THE EAR OF WHEAT

The ear of wheat speaks to us about harvest:
what we sow, and what we reap.
We remember the faithfulness of Ruth
who followed Naomi to her home, and cared for her.
God saw her faithfulness, and rewarded her.
He took her from the edges of the field
and placed her in the master's house –
made her the joy of his heart.

December 17

PSALM 98:4   MICAH 5:2, 4   LUKE 2:15–18

BETHLEHEM

O Bethlehem,
you are but a small village in Judah;
yet you will be the birthplace of my King
who is alive from everlasting ages past!
And He shall stand and feed His flock
in the strength of the Lord,
in the majesty of the name of the Lord our God;
and His people shall remain there undisturbed,
for He will be greatly honoured
all around the world.

He will be our peace.

December 18 Samthann

PSALM 78:70–72; 98:5   I SAMUEL 16:1–12 LUKE 2:8–11, 16, 20

SHEEP

Because the Lord is my shepherd
I have everything that I need.
He lets me rest in fresh meadows,
and leads me along beside quiet streams.
He helps me get better,
and I listen for His call.

December 19

PSALM 98:6   2 CHRONICLES 6:12–15, 18–21   ACTS 7:44–50

THE TEMPLE
Solomon made a home for God –
the most beautiful, the most splendid –
where He could be honoured
and praised
and remembered
and worshipped!
But earth itself or even heaven
could never hold the Almighty
who made them all:
the heavens, the earth,
the temple of Solomon,
could only hold a little
of the glory.

But God Himself
in all His splendour
can squeeze Himself
into a human heart
that is His throne.

December 20

PSALM 98:7 JONAH 1:1–4; 2:10–3:10 MATTHEW 4:16

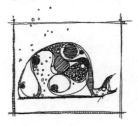

THE WHALE
Where could I run
to get away from You, God?
You've known this game
of hide and seek
for so very long.
At last I give up.
You win.
What was it, this secret
that You wanted me to tell?
The promise:
that You never give up.
You keep on seeking
those who hide from Your love.

December 21

PSALM 72:5–7   ISAIAH 52:7   LUKE 1:26–33, 78–79

PEACE

The prophets said someone was coming
to be the hero all the people needed
to save them, and to champion the weak,
to teach the world about justice
and to bring us all peace.
Isaiah said:
To us a child is born:
we have a son.
He will carry His own throne
on His shoulders.
What are we to call Him?
Wonderful! Counsellor! Mighty God!
The Forever Father!
And for always the Prince of Peace!

December 22

PSALM 98:8–9   ZECHARIAH 4:6–10
MATTHEW 1:12–16; 5:14–16

ZERUBBABEL
Many obstacles stood in his way,
but the time was getting closer.
A longing grew in the hearts of many
to be again a people touched by God.
Zerubbabel was called to be a builder,
but not alone; for many hands must build
a temple for the Lord,
and many hearts determine
to begin the journey,
seek out the ancient paths,
move every mountain in the way.
Only the Spirit of God can bring
the miracle, and let them raise this house:
a beacon of glory on a hill.

December 23

PSALM 72:8–11   JOB 9:9–10   MATTHEW 2:1–2, 7–10

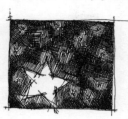

THE STAR

All peoples, all nations shall honour Him.
His love is so great it aches to receive
the homage of every heart.

A star led the travellers to Jesus.
They were seeking for the one life
that could make a difference
in their own lives –
that kind of journey always
changes you for ever.

Jesus, now I've found You,
let me be like that bright star,
showing the way to others
who wonder where You are.

December 24   *Christmas Eve*

PSALM 72:15   ISAIAH 53:10–12   LUKE 2:19, 34–35

CROWN AND SCEPTRE — CROSS AND CROWN
This night, the long night,
the Christ-child will be born –
born to be King, born to die.
Joy comes through the pain –
there is no other way.
Through the long night
we wait in hope.
Cross and crown
bring shadow and light
over this life
who is coming to us.

December 25   *Christmas Day*

PSALM 71:6   ISAIAH 7:14   LUKE 2:4–7

NATIVITY

The virgin is a mother.
The earth can greet her King.
As stumbling shepherds spread the news,
and shimmering angels withdraw in wonder,
the tiny baby searches for her breast.
Mary smiles, and cradles His reality.
Now Jesus is Emmanuel:
heaven's champion is God-in-flesh.
Christmas has come...

December 26 *Stephen*

PSALM 72:14   ISAIAH 63:7–10   ACTS 7:51–60

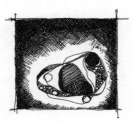

THE STONE

It is an ugly stone, thick and heavy –
but not too heavy to lift, to hurl.
The stone is tinged with red.
We look closely at its shape,
but the crowd does not.
The Christian feels its impact.
The stone is one of many.
His face is raised to heaven
as the stone falls
and he sinks to his knees.
The stones smash his body.
Stephen smiles and sleeps.

December 27 *John the Beloved*

PSALM 71:18–19   HABAKKUK 2:3   JOHN 21:21–25

THE PEN

Mary stored up all these things in her heart
and pondered them. And so did each of us.
And each in our own way told the story.
The story of Jesus can never fully be told.
Each heart He conquers is a new beginning,
and each of us must tell His story;
for His story becomes our own,
even as He has given us His life.

I am the one that Jesus loved.

December 28 *Holy Innocents*

PSALM 71:4   EXODUS 1:15–22   MATTHEW 2:1–3, 12, 16–18

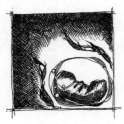

THE FOETUS
Where is the sound of hope,
the cry of a child that wakes?
The dull, aching, continued breathing
of the mother
becomes a wail of grief,
a weeping for the children
who are no more.
The silent landscape shudders.
God of mercy, light in the darkness,
hold gently to Your heart
the tiny ones we cradle in our prayer,
whose life was over
before it had begun.

December 29

PSALM 71:10–12   EXODUS 1:22–2:3   MATTHEW 2:11–15

THE ANGEL

Take the child and His mother down to Egypt's land,
far away from danger, far away from home.
There you may work, there build your Nazareth,
until the time will come when you may return.
Watch well the child who is sleeping now:
the child will be King some day.
Watch well – and we will watch as well.

The child, still sleeping, smiles;
and watching angels wonder, watch and wait.

December 30

PSALM 71:17   HOSEA 11:1   MATTHEW 2:19–23

THE PYRAMIDS

Hidden, journeying across the desert.
Hidden, in a strange place.
Hidden, with the gifts and the prophecies buried.
Their time will come, His time of fulfilment.
These are the days of a carpenter's tools,
a trade that can provide for our needs.
There will be more hidden days, hidden years.
His hands will grow to know the feel of wood,
and weigh the impact of the iron nail.
He must be about His father's business.

But how shall we sing the Lord's song
in a strange and weary land?
In waiting and returning
shall we find rest,
and in quietness and confidence
our strength.

December 31 *John Wycliffe*

PSALM 50:5   I SAMUEL 18:1–4; 20:14–17   LUKE 22:19–20

THE BREAD AND WINE

The covenant is an exchange (even though it be
rags for royalty and royalty for rags).
It is sealed with blood;
the scars of a blood-brother speak of his faithfulness.
The blood-brother has a right to all his brother possesses,
and even the debts become his.
The enemies of one are the enemies of the other.
The blood-brother speaks his promise:
'This is my body; I will lay down my life on your behalf;
and this my blood I willingly shed for you.'

The covenant is exacted with the sharing of a meal,
the promises repeated in the sharing of bread and wine.
'For all of my days, and for all of my life,
I am no longer my own, but yours,
and you are mine.'

fURTbER INfORMATION

Sources and acknowledgements

This book is a reworking of daily readings that have been produced by the Northumbria Community over a number of years.
The original compilation is largely by Andy Raine, as is most
of the revision work – though with assistance from other
Companions in the Community.

Source details have been provided in the text where possible,
but the following provides further information. Permission to
reproduce copyright material is acknowledged with thanks. Every
effort has been made to trace copyright holders, and the authors
and publisher apologize to anyone whose rights have inadvertently not been acknowledged. This will be corrected in any
reprint.

MARCH READINGS

Originally compiled by Andy Raine, and subsequently revised by
Jean-Marc Houssais, drawing on information from *Columbanus
in His Own Words* by Tomas O Fiaich, Veritas Publications,
Dublin, 1974.

APRIL READINGS

Dietrich Bonhoeffer, *Life Together*, translated by John W. Doberstein, SCM Press, London, 1954.
Dietrich Bonhoeffer, *Meditating on the Word*, translation ©1986, 2000 by David Gracie, all rights reserved, and available from Cowley Publications, 28 Temple Place, Boston, MA 02111 (tel 1-800-225-1534; www.cowley.org).
Edwin Robertson, *Bonhoeffer's Heritage*, Hodder & Stoughton, London, 1989.

MAY READINGS

Compiled by Ant and Clare Grimley.
The Wisdom of the Spanish Mystics, compiled by Stephen Glissold, Sheldon Press, London, 1977.

JUNE READINGS

Compiled by Tony Rich.
Athanasius, *The Life of Antony*, translation by R. C. Gregg, Paulist Press, New York, 1980.
The Sayings of the Desert Fathers, translation by Sister Benedicta Ward, Mowbrays, London, 1975.

JULY READINGS

Marion Mill Preminger, *The Sands of Tamanrasset*, Peter Davies, London, 1963.
Charles de Foucauld, *Meditations of a Hermit*, Burns & Oates (a Continuum imprint), London, 1930.
Charles de Foucauld, *Letters from the Desert*, Burns & Oates (a Continuum imprint), London.

AUGUST READINGS

Compiled by Bob and Chris Ainsley.

SEPTEMBER READINGS

Compiled by Tony Rich.
The Sayings of the Desert Fathers, translation by Sister Benedicta Ward, Mowbrays, London, 1975.

OCTOBER READINGS

Reprinted from *Walking on Water: Reflections on Faith and Art* by Madeleine L'Engle © Crosswicks, 1980. Used by permission of Harold Shaw Publishers, Box 567, 388 Gundersen Drive, Wheaton, Illinois, U.S.A. 60189. (This book is highly commended to those interested in the life of the Spirit in the work of a writer, or artist of any kind.)

NOVEMBER READINGS

Gilbert Shaw, *A Pilgrim's Book of Prayers*, SLG, London, 1992.

DECEMBER READINGS

Text by Andy Raine.
Line illustrations © 2000 Sara Bennett-Steele.

The Northumbria Community

The Northumbria Community in its present form emerged as an expression of the mixed life that embraces both the contemplative and the apostolic in the context of a shared vision and vocation. Historically, Celtic Christian monasticism was noted for its combining of monastery and mission. Ordinary Christian people found ways of weaving disciplines of prayer into their daily lives. We were aware from the earliest days of this call to a continuity of purpose which would enable us to help 'rebuild the ancient ruins and raise up the age-old foundations' of our fore-fathers and -mothers in the faith. We were being drawn slowly into a monastic way, but this was a new and different monasticism. Dietrich Bonhoeffer spoke of a similar call when he wrote, 'The renewal of the Church will come from a new type of monasticism which only has in common with the old an uncompromising allegiance to the Sermon on the Mount. It is high time people banded together to do this.'

This understanding of people united by a common vision was central to our formation as a geographically dispersed Community. In effect, two groups came together: the one emphasizing the monastic, contemplative stream; and the other emphasizing the apostolic and the need to take the monastery through mission into the marketplace. The merging of the two groups in 1990 formed the Northumbria Community. In our growth and development we have gradually understood that, for us, this being 'banded together' was expressed in being alone yet together, enriched by our diversity, but united in heart by our common commitment to our vows of saying 'Yes' to Availability and Vulnerability, and in being companions together in Community.

Since the Community is widely dispersed, Community groups have been established, meeting monthly, wherever companions in a local area wish to form one. Inevitably these take on a life and form of their own, and each individual contributes to the wide variety of experience and styles of a disparate group of people finding themselves on a journey together.

Friendship, and sharing of stories, music and the arts in general, all provide the natural means to help us engage with people of all backgrounds and interests in a manner that leaps across the boundaries of church and religion. In recent months we have paid special attention to encouraging those with an interest in story-telling, and to teaching the skills that make it such an effective bridge-building tool.

Our trading company, Cloisters, has a mail-order business selling calligraphic cards, stained-glass ornaments, honey from the Community's beehives, etc., and is developing music and book publishing activities to enable the stories and insights to be passed on to a wider audience. This reflects the desert tradition of 'basket-making' and helps raise funds for the Community.

In carrying out these activities, we are very concerned that the Community does not become institutionalized. The rather anonymous, raw and ragged style of the early part of the journey remains a vital part of the Community's ethos as it grows and develops. We aspire to measure ourselves constantly against these words of William Stringfellow, which have long been an inspiration to us: 'Dynamic and erratic, spontaneous and radical, audacious and immature, committed if not altogether coherent. Ecumenically open and often experimental; visible here and there, now and then, but unsettled institutionally. Almost monastic in nature, but most of all enacting a fearful hope for society.'

THE COMMUNITY RULE OF AVAILABILITY AND VULNERABILITY

In the same way that the liturgies in *Celtic Daily Prayer* emerged from lives actually lived in community, so has the Community's Rule. It is a response to that insistent question: 'How then shall we live?' It is a call to *risky* living: it is not a comfortable or easy solution to life's problems. Whilst we welcome any who wish to walk with us in seeking God, we ask that those who wish to become Companions with us in Community say 'Yes' to

Availability and Vulnerability as their way of living. This involves availability to God and to others – expressed in a commitment to being alone with God in the cell of our own heart and to being available for hospitality, intercession and mission. Intentional vulnerability is expressed through being teachable in the discipline of prayer, saturated in the Scriptures and accountable to one another, often through soul friendships. It also means 'embracing the heretical imperative' (challenging assumed truth), being receptive to constructive criticism, affirming that relationships matter more than reputation, and living openly among people as church 'without walls'. This is not something to be entered into lightly!

286 CELTIC DAILY READINGS

Contacting the Community

The Northumbria Community can make the following available:

* Information pack
* Regular Prayer Guide
* Programme of retreats and teaching at The Nether Springs at Hetton Hall
* *Caim* – the Community's quarterly newsletter
* Catalogues of Cloisters products including the musical versions, on CD and audiotape, of the Daily Offices and Complines
* Information about Storytelling
* Information about Gift Aid payments to the Community
* Information about tax-exempt giving in the USA

Please use the contact details below:

The Northumbria Community
Hetton Hall
Chatton
Northumberland
NE66 5SD
UK

tel: 01289 388235 (from outside UK: #44 1289 388235)
fax: 01289 388510 (from outside UK: #44 1289 388510)
email: northumbriacommunity@bigfoot.com
website: www.northumbriacommunity.org

The Northumbria Community Trust Ltd
IPS No 28305R
An exempt charity registered in England and Wales

QUICK REFERENCE GUIDE

Advent: pp. xiv–xv; December (pp. 247–279)
Aidan: January 25 (p. 20)
Antony: p. xiii; June (pp. 109–134)

Bonhoeffer, Dietrich: p. xiii; April 11–15 (pp. 79–83)
Brendan: April 28–29 (pp. 94–5)
Brigid: April 16 (p. 84)

de Foucauld, Charles: p. xiii; July (pp. 135–166)

Christmas: December 24, 25 (pp. 272–3)
Colman: pp. x–xii; January 28 (p. 23); April 20 (p. 86)
Columba: January 13 (p. 10); April 1 (p. 72); April 18, 19
(pp. 85–6)
Columbanus: p.xiii; March (pp. 48–71); April 27 (p. 94)
Comgall: January 2 (p. 2)

Death and dying: April 21 (p. 87); April 24 (p. 90); June 26 (p. 130)
Doherty, Catherine de Hueck: January 9 (p. 7); February 23, 24
(p. 41)

Epiphany ('twelfth night'): January 1 (p. 1); December 23 (p. 271)

Francis of Assisi: February 25 (p. 42)

Gall: March 9–11 (pp. 55–7); March 14 (p. 59); March 21 (p. 64)

Holy Innocents: December 28 (p. 276)

John of the Cross: pp. xiii–xiv; January 21 (p. 17); p. 96; May 4 (p. 97); May 6 (p. 98); May 13 (p. 101); May 25 (p. 106); May 27 (p. 107); May 31 (p. 108)
John the Beloved: January 28 (p. 23), December 27 (p. 275)

Mary, mother of Jesus: October 2, 3 (pp. 211–2); December 25 (p. 273); December 27 (p. 275); December 29–30 (pp. 277–8)
Michael and all angels: February 8 (p. 31); November 7 (p. 230)
Mid-life: February 18 (p. 39)

New Year: December 31 (p. 279)
Ninian: November 11 (p. 232)

Patrick: November 10 (p. 231)
Pentecost: p. vii
Polycarp: March 25 (p. 66)

Stephen: January 16 (p. 13); December 19 (p. 267); December 26 (p. 274)

Teresa of Avila: pp. xiii–xiv; January 19 (p. 16); p. 96; May 2 (p. 97); May 5 (p. 98); May 10, 11 (p. 100); May 17 (p. 103); May 21, 22 (pp. 104–5); May 24 (p. 106)

Way of the Cross: February 17 (p. 39); December 21 (p. 269)
Wilfrid: January 28 (p. 23)